# TRAITOR

The Whistleblower
and
the "American Taliban"

Jesselyn Radack

The following memoir is constructed from what I (and others with whom I conferred) can remember and is my opinion, perspective, and analysis.

Previously published as *The Canary in the Coalmine*

ISBN: 978-0-9839928-0-6

LCCN: 2011938062

## DEDICATION

To my husband, Daniel, who walked beside me on the dark path of whistleblowers and shone a flashlight to illuminate my way. I also dedicate this to Jacob, Sam, and Tenlea, in hopes that by writing about this they should never have to live through anything similar.

# CONTENTS

# ACKNOWLEDGMENTS

Thank you to my attorneys, Rick Robinson, Mona Lyons, and Bruce Fein for protecting my interests. Thanks also to Ray McGovern and Suz Kreuger who underwrote the original version of this book, and for Suz and Jamie Kreuger's help in bringing it to life. I owe a debt of gratitude to Marsha Foss and Dick Bell for their superb editing skills the first time around, and to Laura Sarasqueta for this edition.

Thanks to Ben Baker and Beth Adelson for their photography, and to M. Graciela Steiger for keeping me sane. I appreciate the enormous talents of the 1106 Design team for shepherding the second edition of this book.

The silver lining to this case is all the wonderful people it brought into my life—Jane Mayer, Tony Lewis, Eric Lichtblau, Coleen Rowley, Daniel Ellsberg, Ted Kennedy, Bruce Fein, Mike German, and the many others I have doubtless left out. These people were my heroes, and many became professional colleagues as well as friends.

# FOREWORD

## By Glenn Greenwald

THE OBAMA ADMINISTRATION is steadfastly protecting from prosecution—or judicial review of any kind—the high-level government officials who systematically broke the law during the Bush administration. Torture is one of the most glaring examples of this lawbreaking. In June 2002, Jesselyn Radack exposed one of the first cases of torture post-9/11—being used on an American—in the case of John Walker Lindh. Her sobering book should be required reading for all first-ycar law students because it shows poignantly how "national security" is being used to fundamentally bastardize constitutional law, criminal procedure, human rights, civil liberties and legal ethics. As a Justice Department attorney, she advised that an American terrorism suspect should be afforded the right to counsel, one of the most basic tenets of our criminal justice system. When her advice was disregarded and then "disappeared," she blew the whistle.

Government overzealousness and misconduct caused the Bush administration's first high-profile terrorism prosecution after 9/11 to implode, and the government punished Radack unmercifully—putting her under a criminal "leak" investigation, referring her to the state bars in which she's licensed as an attorney, and putting her on the "No-Fly" List. But it took the Obama administration to actually *prosecute* whistleblowers, and all six (more such prosecutions than have occurred in all previous Administrations combined) have been charged under the draconian, World War I-era Espionage Act.

As a candidate, Obama had this to say about whistleblowers: "Often the best source of information about waste, fraud, and abuse in government is an existing government employee committed to public integrity and willing to speak out. Such acts of courage and patriotism, which can sometimes save lives and often save taxpayer dollars, should be encouraged rather than stifled." Apparently, by "encouraged," he meant: "snuffed out with relentless prosecution and intimidation."

The Obama administration has prosecuted more whistleblowers for allegedly mishandling classified information than all previous presidents combined. When former senior NSA official Thomas Drake was indicted back in April 2010, I wrote at the time: ". . .the more I think about this, the more I think this might actually be one of the worst steps the Obama administration has taken yet, if not the single worst step—and that's obviously saying a lot." The effect of prosecuting Drake with multiple "espionage" counts, threatening him with decades in prison, and financially ruining him is clear: to frighten future whistleblowers into silence, and thus enable the government and the National Security State to do whatever it wants free of one of the only true checks it has. That's what makes Obama's War on Whistleblowing so pernicious.

The motive for the Obama Justice Department's broader war on whistleblowers is to send a "message" of intimidation to future would-be whistleblowers. The Obama Justice Department intimidates and deters future whistleblowers from exposing what they know, thus further suffocating one of the very few remaining mechanisms

America has to learn about what takes place behind the virtually impenetrable Wall of Secrecy—a Wall of Secrecy that the Obama administration, through its promiscuous use of "state secrets" and immunity claims, has relentlessly fortified and expanded. For anyone who is engaged in meaningful dissent from and challenge to government officials—the Jim Risens and other real investigative reporters, the Thomas Drakes and other whistleblowers, the WikiLeaks supporters, the Midwest peace activists—these prosecutions and these ever-expanding surveillance, detention and even assassination powers are inevitably intimidating. Regardless of how those powers are used or even whether they are, they will, as Risen put it, have "a chilling effect" on the exercise of core freedoms.

Adding insult to injustice, you have the Obama Justice Department bringing no prosecutions (but rather full-scale immunity extended) for war crimes, torture, and illegal spying. For those crimes, we must *Look Forward, Not Backward*. But for those poor individuals who courageously blow the whistle on oozing corruption, waste and illegal surveillance by the omnipotent public-private Surveillance State: the full weight of the "justice system" comes crashing down upon them with threats of many years in prison.

Just marvel at the Kafkaesque authoritarian mentality that produces government statements like this from the CIA: "Just because something is in the public domain doesn't mean it's been officially released or declassified by the U.S. government." The State Department has issued a nearly-identical statement that "unauthorized disclosure of classified documents in the media (print, blog, website) does not mean that the documents have been declassified." Someone can be censored, or even prosecuted and imprisoned, for discussing "classified" information that has long been in the public domain. But as absurd as it is, this deceitful scheme—suppressing embarrassing information or evidence of illegality by claiming that even public information is "classified"—is standard government practice for punishing whistle-blowers and other critics and shielding high-level lawbreakers. Even worse, often the "classified" information is not properly categorized. As J. William Leonard, the classification czar under Bush, said of the Drake case, "I've never seen a more deliberate and willful example of government officials improperly classifying a document." After all the government's hysterical theatrics, the federal judges in both the Radack and Drake cases found they disclosed only *unclassified* information to the media.

A close cousin of rampant overclassification, the Obama DOJ has continuously claimed that victims of the U.S. rendition, torture and eavesdropping programs cannot have their claims litigated in court because what was done to them are "state secrets"—even when what was done to them has long been publicly known and even formally, publicly investigated and litigated in open court in other countries. Far more often than anything else, the real purpose of government secrecy is to shield ineptitude, corruption, abuse of power and illegality from seeing the light of day, and to ensure that the government controls what the public hears and what it does not hear.

Ironically, it is that behavior—abusing secrecy powers to cover-up embarrassing and incriminating evidence—that is a far more destructive and common crime than the unauthorized leaks. As the Supreme Court explained in rejecting Nixon's classified-based censorship efforts of the Pentagon Papers: "The dominant purpose of the First Amendment was to prohibit the widespread practice of governmental suppression of embarrassing information." Indeed, abusing secrecy powers to conceal embarrassing and incriminating information has long been illegal. Abusing government secrecy powers is a vastly more frequent and damaging illegal act than unauthorized leaks, yet the president obsesses on the latter while doing virtually nothing about the former other than continuing its worst manifestations. As the Supreme Court explained, few things are more damaging to a democracy than allowing political leaders to abuse secrecy powers to cover-up wrongdoing and control the flow of information the public hears; i.e., to propagandize the citizenry.

But that's exactly what Washington's secrecy fixation is designed to achieve. And while excessive secrecy has been a problem in the U.S. for decades, the Obama administration's unprecedented war on whistleblowers makes it much more odious, since it is about not only keeping vital information from the public and stifling public debate, but also threatening whistleblowers (and investigative reporters) with prolonged imprisonment. That's why they turn what candidate Obama called these "acts of courage and patriotism" (whistleblowing) into crimes, while the real criminals—political officials who abuse their secrecy powers for corrupted, self-interested ends—go unpunished.

The poetic justice of Radack's appalling experience is that she is using her hard-learned lessons to advocate for and represent some of today's biggest whistleblowers: Thomas Drake, Bradley Manning, Peter Van Buren, and John Doe in *Doe v. Rumsfeld*. As Drake put it: "Jesselyn truly became my public voice and conscience—speaking out and writing fearlessly and courageously—bringing truth to power with all her simply superb outreach and advocacy. I am incredibly grateful for all that she has done for me as a whistleblower, and the totality of her efforts and actions that so immensely helped in achieving a huge and decisive victory against an implacable government prosecution—and thereby keeping me free."

# SHOOT THE MESSENGER

I AM THE DEPARTMENT OF JUSTICE ATTORNEY who blew the whistle on government misconduct in the case of John Walker Lindh, the "American Taliban."

Everyone remembers the indelible trophy photo of the "American Taliban"—one of the most prominent prisoners of the Afghan war—naked, blindfolded, tied up, and bound to a board. That was our first glimpse of American-sponsored torture and we didn't even flinch. Lindh was found barely alive, shot in the leg, and suffering from dehydration, hypothermia, and frostbite. Although Lindh was in critical condition, US soldiers threatened to kill him, stripped him, blindfolded and trussed him, scrawled "shithead" across the blindfold, duct-taped him to a board for days in an unheated and unlit shipping container, and posed with him for pictures. Parts of his ordeal were captured on videotape. Sound familiar?

The Lindh case was a harbinger of what would occur on a much larger scale at the American-run Abu Ghraib prison in Iraq and elsewhere. Like an aggressive, contagious, deadly virus, this first outbreak of lawless behavior was spread by the CIA and Army intelligence teams to the entire archipelago of American-controlled detention centers throughout the world. The scandal is not, in former President George W. Bush's words, the "disgraceful conduct by a few" bad apples, or in former Secretary of Defense Donald Rumsfeld's words, the "grievous and brutal abuse and cruelty at the hands of a few members of the United States armed forces." It's that the Bush administration thought it could torture people and get away with it, which—as I update this memoir a decade later—they essentially have, thanks to their refusal to police themselves and President Barack Obama's "Look Forward, Not Backward" posture toward war crimes, torture, and warrantless wiretapping.

As a thirty-year-old Justice Department attorney and legal ethics advisor, I recommended against interrogating "American Taliban" John Walker Lindh without his lawyer and, later, blew the whistle when evidence of my advice was destroyed and withheld from the court. The Justice Department forced me out of my job, placed me under criminal investigation, got me fired from my next job in the private sector, reported me to the state bars in which I'm licensed as a lawyer, and put me on the "No-Fly" list.

I don't wear the label "whistleblower" comfortably. Why should I get some special moniker for doing what I would have done anyway? The vast majority of civil servants labeled as "whistleblowers" rarely think of themselves in that role. In their minds, they were simply doing their jobs. Increasingly, the line between simply doing what is right and being a whistleblower has become blurred, particularly as society changes its expectations about how government employees should serve the public.

Yet our nation's top leaders pay lip service to the importance of whistleblowers. After his election, President Barack Obama's transition agenda said it was a priority to protect whistleblowers:

Often the best source of information about waste, fraud, and abuse in government is an existing government employee committed to public integrity and willing to speak out. Such acts of courage and patriotism, which can sometimes save lives and often save taxpayer dollars, should be encouraged rather than stifled. We need to empower federal employees as watchdogs of wrongdoing and partners in performance.

But the conscientious employee is not welcome by presidencies of either stripe; in fact, Obama has been worse than Bush—something to keep in mind as the following pages are read.

Our country has a love-hate relationship with whistleblowers. When one thinks of a whistleblower, images from movies such as *The Insider* or *Erin Brokovich* spring to mind; so do Coleen Rowley of the FBI, Sherron Watkins of Enron, and Cynthia Cooper of WorldCom, who were *TIME Magazine's* "Persons of the Year" in 2002, when whistleblowers enjoyed a rare moment of admiration. One has visions of determined individuals risking it all to make explosive disclosures before Congress or on "60 Minutes." The media glorifies those who risk everything to expose corruption and illegal activity and rightly so; these lionized individuals deserve every ounce of praise they receive. But their happy outcomes are not typical—for every success story, there are a hundred stories of professional martyrdom. Mine is one of them.

Few paths are more treacherous than the one that challenges abuse of power and tries to make a meaningful difference. Whistleblowers often find that they become the subject of the story. Any personal vulnerability they possess can, and will, be used against them and, through these smears, the whistleblower's charges become a subordinate issue. The Bush administration was expert at this subterfuge.

The conscientious employee is often portrayed as vengeful, unstable, or out for attention or profit. I have not been completely immune from such accusations, but the terms that have been used by "anonymous Justice Department officials" to describe me are far more incendiary: "traitor," "turncoat," and "terrorist sympathizer." Never mind that in debate circles, the lowest form of argumentation is name-calling. For an administration attempting to quell opposition through a campaign of secrecy and silence, neither the Bush White House nor the Ashcroft Justice Department were short of words.

One of the Bush administration's favorite tactics was to paint any sort of dissent or criticism—whether it came from whistleblowers, anti-war protesters, or advocates of the politically unpopular—as disloyal at best and unpatriotic at worst. With a crusader's fervor, Ashcroft warned in stark terms that critics who "scare peace-loving people with phantoms of lost liberty . . . only aid terrorists, for they erode our national unity and diminish our resolve." The reverse actually proved true. The government's fear-mongering among the populace became a frequent and effective tool to usurp freedom and divide Americans in the name of national security and in the guise of fighting terrorists. In a ham-handed way, Ashcroft tried to portray the expression and exercise of civil liberties as treasonous. Such ill-considered exhortations have a very real, very chilling effect on the exercise of basic freedom of speech. The idea that you have to trade civil liberties for national security is a false dichotomy that its proponents should be ashamed to advance.

Although my story is different in its details, it shares many of the same elements with the experiences of other whistleblowers: abuse of government power, lack of due process (or any process at all), secrecy, political overkill, and pure retaliation. The Bush administration's vindictive response to its critics went beyond questioning their truthfulness, competence, and motives. It sought to destroy their careers and livelihoods. I never could have imagined that President Obama would take it one step further; trying to put them in jail.

In most cases of whistleblowing, the executive branch attacks the person rather than the substance of his or her complaint. It shoots the messenger rather than addressing the message. It silences the critic rather than answering the criticism. It engages in intimidation, character assassination, and career destruction of those who break the code of silence. And it will not let go. As Jerome Doolittle, novelist and former White House speechwriter, characterized the Justice Department's venomous attacks on me: "There is something primordial about Team Bush's reaction to dissent, something reptilian. They're like the gila monster, its jaws holding their poisonous grip even after its head is severed." If the Bush administration was primordial, the Obama administration is downright pathological—and I'm saying this as someone who campaigned for, contributed to, and voted for Obama.

"You are either with us or against us"—Bush's Procrustean mantra during his inexorable march to the war in Iraq—applied with even greater force to those who crossed him and, more broadly, to anyone he perceived as an "enemy." Ashcroft shared Bush's us-or-them mentality, and their binary thinking became reflected in the deep division between "Red America" and "Blue America," shorthand for Republicans and Democrats. Bush and Ashcroft also shared a limitless capacity to nurse incandescent grudges. Ashcroft made clear that forgiveness, while perfectly appropriate in religion, had no place at the Justice Department (except for the Department's own officials who broke the law.) "The law is not about forgiveness," he said. "It is oftentimes about vengeance, oftentimes about revenge."

One of the most disturbing things about my story is that it's not an isolated incident. As bizarre, unbelievable, and outrageous as it sounds, it is not uncommon and has only worsened under Obama. These vicissitudes have happened to everyone from military officers to Muslims playing paintball. It has even happened to other Justice Department attorneys, such as Thomas Tamm.

I've decided to tell my story because I vowed that if I could ever speak safely again, I would not remain silent out of some sort of misplaced gratitude that I was no longer being threatened with termination, criminal prosecution, disbarment, or blacklisting.

My ordeal should have been able to end at many junctures along the trajectory. I was muzzled for over a year, so I have a lot of pent-up things to say. Also, I feel a moral imperative to say them because if people understand how a person like me who enjoys relative privilege—being white, a US citizen, educated, and comfortably middle-class—can so easily lose her freedom, then maybe people in this country can more easily understand the plight of those in post-9/11 America who are Arab or Muslim, who are immigrants, who are poor, or who don't speak English. Ironically, the role I played for which I suffered my loss of freedoms was downplayed by the very officials who worked so hard to strip them from me. As then-CBS commentator Andrew Cohen noted:

> It was clear, although the government never explicitly conceded so, that prosecutors were open to a [plea bargain] deal with Lindh because of the brutal way in which he was treated by his military captors in Afghanistan and the spurious way in which federal law enforcement officials had observed Lindh's constitutional rights. It is no coincidence that the Lindh deal came about on the eve of a scheduled week-long [suppression] hearing that was going to bring into the open the specifics of how Lindh was treated and by whom.

Cohen, too, got a dose of government petulance for his efforts. In a classic case of "the lady doth protest too much," top officials at Justice took time out of their busy schedules to call him after his article ran to try to convince him that he was wrong; specifically, that I had *not* caused the Lindh case to implode. They minimized me and downplayed my role in Lindh's surprise plea bargain.

If I really had nothing to do with the unraveling of the Lindh case (in the words of investigative journalist Jane Mayer, "the prosecution collapsed"), then query why Ashcroft and his functionaries wasted so much time, energy, and taxpayer money "getting back at" me. If I were a crank making wild allegations about the Lindh case, I would have been ignored. But when the assistant attorney general starts throwing his weight around to keep me quiet, you have to wonder what I know.

Whether I played a large role or none at all, the government severely damaged my reputation and my psyche. It's hard to un-ring the bell. One person against an entire agency or government is a David versus Goliath struggle. In terms of raw power, the government holds all the cards. To sic the infinite resources of the United States government on someone is more than a mismatched contest—it is tyranny. It is also a tremendous waste of what we are reminded time and again are precious and limited government resources.

It has been hard for me to write this memoir because I suffer from the imperative of objectivity—the mistaken belief that impartiality will lend credibility to my story. But how can I be neutral when what I have experienced has been so personal and so driven by emotion, surmise, and partisan politics? I therefore confess up front that I have an ax to grind and nearly $100,000 in legal bills to show for it.

I'm here to tell you that the emperor has no clothes and that those who expose the nakedness of government policies and practices should be applauded, not annihilated. Public service does not mean blind obedience to one's boss or subservience to an agency agenda that subverts the law and the public interest. Deciding to blow the whistle can be the single most important decision an individual ever makes. It should not be a question of whether to blow the whistle, but of how loudly to blow it. And in doing so, public servants should not be forced to choose their conscience over their career.

The years immediately following 9/11 were the most difficult of my life, but they were also a cataclysmic growth period that cemented my commitment to civil liberties and human rights, and the whistle-blowers who risked their careers to preserve them. I fully realize that there are many stories like mine and that I am just a footnote in a seismic shift toward secrecy that has been growing in our country. However, I promised myself that if I could ever speak freely again, then I would use my voice to try to prevent this sort of political silencing from happening to anyone else.

A lot of commentators saw the John Walker Lindh case as an example of the government going after a minnow with a sledgehammer, and the same can be said for my case writ small. My saga, as did the life-altering journeys of so many others, began on September 11, 2001.

# MAIN JUSTICE

'M AN ATTORNEY, although I am so disgusted by the behavior of some of the lawyers in my ordeal that I've been tempted to leave the profession and join the ranks of other recovering lawyers. But then I'd be giving the wrongdoers exactly what they want: for me to quit the practice of law.

In 1995, I graduated from Yale Law School and joined the Department of Justice through the Attorney General's Honors Program. At the time, the prestigious Honors Program was the recruitment mechanism for entry-level attorneys and the only mechanism through which the Department hired graduating law students. Nearly 5,000 budding lawyers from around the country applied for approximately 150 slots. A whopping third of my class applied to the Program. The Civil Division hired two of us from the class of '95.

That same year, a politician named John Ashcroft became the junior senator from Missouri. A devout member of the Assemblies of God, a Pentecostal denomination, Ashcroft routinely likened his political career to the life and death of Jesus, referring to his campaign victories as "resurrections" and his political defeats as "crucifixions."

This was a resurrection. As described in his 1998 book, *Lessons From a Father to His Son*, Ashcroft's friends anointed him with Crisco oil from the kitchen, marking his ascension in the style of "the ancient kings of Israel."

The Honors Program had long been viewed as a premier opportunity for rookie lawyers—a plum assignment—and it was definitely my dream job. The Program offered excellent trial advocacy training, an opportunity to serve the public, and the chance to actually see the inside of a courtroom much sooner than if I had had to pay my dues in the suffocating library of some law firm. Just as importantly for me, it guaranteed health and life insurance—coverage I could not obtain privately because I have multiple sclerosis, a chronic neurological disease also known as a "preexisting medical condition," a daunting reality for a twenty-four-year-old.

Little did I know that the Honors Program, founded by President Eisenhower's first attorney general and long overseen by career attorneys, would later be hijacked by Ashcroft and his acolytes as part of a broader politicization of the Justice Department. When I started, the Honors Program was highly competitive, well regarded, and had the laudable distinction of being apolitical.

Ashcroft decided in 2002 that the Program would benefit from more direct participation by him and other political appointees. He created a three-member Steering Committee to screen candidates' applications. None on the Steering Committee had ever served as an attorney in any of the Department's litigating divisions and they improperly allowed applicants' political and ideological affiliations to guide their decision-making, in violation of Department policies, civil service laws, and various federal criminal laws. Michael Elston, one of the Steering Committee members, later showed his stripes in the mass firing scandal of at least six US attorneys in 2006. He called one of the ousted attorneys, Bud Cummins, to ominously warn him that the Justice Department would view any kind of public criticism by the fired US attorneys "as a major escalation of conflict meriting some kind of unspecified form of retaliation," as if being summarily fired for no reason was not enough reprisal.

I joined the Department of Justice's Civil Division and practiced constitutional tort litigation for four years. In plain English, that means I defended the United States and individual federal officials against allegations of constitutional and statutory violations. But the so-called *Bivens* section, jokingly referred to by my future husband as the "vivisection" for its unforgiving hours and volatile directors, became incompatible with my life as it evolved beyond the office. The icing on the cake of my courtroom days was a federal jury trial in a godforsaken locale while I was seven-months pregnant with our second son, Sam. I won the trial, but afterward all that the jurors wanted to know was whether I was having a boy or a girl, when the baby was due, and whether or not my co-counsel (who had the same last name) was my brother or my husband (he was neither). I took it as a sign that it was time to leave litigation.

Luckily, during the preceding seven months I had been detailed part-time to the Justice Department's newly created Professional Responsibility Advisory Office (PRAO), which renders ethics advice to Department attorneys nationwide. The office was established after passage of the McDade Amendment, a law that subjected Department of Justice attorneys to not only their own state bar rules, but also the bar rules of any state in which they litigated. This statute created vertical and horizontal conflicts of law because most Department attorneys have a multi-jurisdictional practice and are licensed in more than one bar.

I found legal ethics fascinating, challenging, and important, and being a legal advisor offered me an opportunity to leave behind the travel, deadlines, and general acrimony of litigation. Moreover, it was rare and exciting in a calcified bureaucracy like the Department of Justice to be a part of a fledgling office in its infancy, rather than one that was entrenched, as most were.

After my maternity leave, I started as a full-time legal advisor at PRAO on Valentine's Day of 2000. There were three layers of security for Department attorneys—"Confidential," "Secret," and "Top Secret"—before the massive proliferation of hybrid secrecy categories that followed 9/11. This position required a Top Secret clearance. I soon underwent my five-year background re-investigation, which I passed easily. I had always tried to be ethically meticulous while working for the Department of Justice. I remembered vividly that, during law school, Zoë Baird, the wife of one of my professors, had lost her chance to become the first female attorney general because she neglected to pay taxes for her household help. I was fastidious about properly paying our "nanny taxes," even though I knew many Justice colleagues—attorneys, no less—who did not. Now that I was working at PRAO, the "ethics office," I felt that it was even more incumbent upon me to do things by the book.

PRAO was housed in the National Theatre Building—a fancy office space by government standards. At lunch I could go skating at Pershing Park Ice Rink across the street, an added bonus for a former figure skater. I loved my new job and seemed to have a knack for legal ethics.

The newly hired director, Claudia Flynn, was a very astute and together-looking woman. Her elegant stature, fiery red hair, flawless makeup, and immaculate dress made her striking. We had gone to the same college, so we immediately shared that bond. I really looked up to her.

Much to my delight, in September, Claudia gave me a $2000 cash performance award, signaling that I had excelled during my first seven months as a permanent attorney at PRAO. With Claudia's backing, I started writing a law review article on the unintended consequences of the McDade Amendment, the legislation that was the impetus for our office and, as would turn out to be a stinging irony for me, that was meant to curb overzealous prosecutors. *The Georgetown Journal of Legal Ethics*, the nation's premiere legal ethics periodical and the only law journal to which PRAO subscribed, accepted the article for publication.

In January 2001, Larry Thompson, a former US attorney then in private practice in Atlanta, published an article on how the McDade Amendment was *good* for the profession—a position 180 degrees opposite from the one PRAO took and that I took in my article. In February, it became public that President Bush intended to appoint Thompson, an African-American, to be deputy attorney general, a move designed in part to deflect criticism that Ashcroft (chosen by President Bush to score points with social conservatives) was insensitive to race. For example, Ashcroft had given the 1999 commencement address at Bob Jones University, a fundamentalist institution that, until 2000, upheld and defended distinctly racist policies. As a senator, he had also denied the first black Missouri Supreme Court justice, Ronnie White, a federal judgeship for being "pro-criminal," when Ashcroft's real grudge was that White had outsmarted him by defeating a draconian anti-abortion measure.

A draft of my law review article was in Thompson's briefing book, which was provided to him to prepare for his confirmation hearing. In March, I sent him the latest version of the article because I knew it took a position on the McDade Amendment—that the law had hampered federal prosecutors in carrying out their duties—that was diametrically opposed to his. I also knew that three senators on the Judiciary Committee had introduced proposals to amend McDade and that Thompson would be quizzed about it.

Before his hearing, Thompson called me at home to discuss the McDade Amendment. He had not realized it was complicating the job of Department attorneys. We became email buddies of sorts during the unsettling months leading up to his confirmation. I think he was just venting from the stress of it all and I was a sympathetic ear. Sure enough, during the confirmation hearing, he was grilled by Senator Patrick Leahy, ranking Democrat on the Judiciary Committee, about the McDade Amendment and was able to deftly respond that he had only recently learned of the problems it was causing for Justice attorneys. In early May, he was confirmed and sworn in.

He invited me to lunch in June. One of his associate deputy attorneys general, David Kris (later Obama's National Security Advisor at Justice), told me it was a huge deal to make it onto Larry Thompson's schedule. I was just before Paul O'Neill, the Secretary of Treasury. Kris also recommended that I be open with Claudia about how cozy I was becoming with Larry (we were on a first-name basis by then), especially since it could lead to a job change for me.

I told Claudia about my budding friendship with Larry and my upcoming lunch with him. I also told her that I would be interested in doing a detail to his office or seeking a political appointment. She seemed surprised, but supportive. On June 14, Larry and I shared a delightful lunch in his new office and discussed the possibility of my serving as his counsel.

People often ask me if I felt a big shift from the Janet Reno Justice Department to the one run by Ashcroft. The answer is, not at first. It is true that Ashcroft preferred a corporate "top-down" model and valued secrecy, which stood in stark contrast to Reno's general policy of *glasnost* and her reputation for endless briefings. However, Ashcroft's style was in keeping with Bush's strict code of loyalty and Rumsfeld's "command climate." Also, a chilly relationship developed between Ashcroft's political denizens and career Justice attorneys.

The Ashcroft hires were suspicious of the career attorneys, thought they were too liberal, and effectively cut them out of many important policy-making decisions.

But for the most part, Ashcroft, humbled by the humiliating loss of his Senate seat (he lost to Missouri Governor Mel Carnahan, who had died *before* the election) and a bruising confirmation fight (he had received forty-two negative votes, the most ever cast against a nominee for attorney general), seemed content to lay low, host early-morning prayer gatherings on government property, and quietly serve as Bush's symbolic ambassador to the right.

For me, the sea change was not so much with the change in administration, but rather with September 11, 2001, which changed the lives of everyone in our country and created a revolution inside the Justice Department. On that fateful morning, Ashcroft and four aides were on a government plane en route to Milwaukee when a call came in on Ashcroft's secure phone line. He hung up and announced, "Our world has changed forever."

John Ashcroft changed, too. Before September 11, he couldn't have cared less about terrorism. Four months before the diabolical attacks, he didn't even *mention* terrorism in outlining priorities for the Justice Department. But September 11 emboldened him and opened the door to reshaping the Justice Department. He went from being embattled and disengaged to being a man on a mission. The detached and sedate Ashcroft was replaced by a defiant, pugnacious, and polarizing zealot who dove into the war on terrorism with an enthusiasm that made his fierce opposition to abortion and gun control look like Victorian high tea. His draping of the female "Spirit of Justice" statue was not just a puritanical act; it was a metaphorical one.

# 9/11 AND THE FALL

CLAUDIA GRABBED ME from my office on her way upstairs to watch the conference room TV. A plane had just flown into one of the World Trade Center towers. On the screen was a live broadcast of smoke streaming from the tower, a marked contrast against the clear and cerulean sky. The handful of us who had gathered all thought it was a freak mishap. As we watched in real-time, a twin-engine Boeing going 400 miles an hour slammed into the other tower, exiting the opposite side in a flaming ball that created a torrential downpour of fiery debris. In a collective gasp, all doubt was removed—this was no accident.

We all took turns calling our significant others on the conference room phone. No one wanted to stray from the TV. I called Dan. He was still at home with the kids and completely unaware of what had happened.

"Dan, turn on the TV. Two planes just flew into the World Trade Center! They think it's terrorism. Don't take Jacob to nursery school yet."

Barbara Olson, a passenger on American Airlines Flight 77, phoned her husband, Solicitor General Theodore Olson, in the Justice Department. She told him that her plane had been hijacked. Twenty minutes later, the sprawling glass windows facing Pennsylvania Avenue rattled and a dull boom shook the room—the percussive effect of a 757 out of Dulles slamming into the Pentagon. We watched out the panoramic windows as people started streaming into the street below. Within minutes, a plume of rufous smoke silhouetted the Washington Monument.

Claudia said that we could leave. But it was unclear if we would be any better off in the growing chaos outside the building than in its comparatively safe confines. The FAA had shut down the air traffic system across the country, but the news reported that some planes were still in the air. At least inside we had access to phones, computers, radios, a TV, and water. Moreover, getting home sounded like a logistical nightmare. The news reported that the Metro was not running and that the bridges leaving DC were closed.

Just then, the south tower of the World Trade Center telescoped into the street, creating a massive noxious cloud of powder, debris, and smoke. We watched open-mouthed.

Down the street, Secret Service agents armed with automatic weapons deployed into Lafayette Park across from the White House. The TV reported a car bomb at the State Department. We heard a tremendous explosion.

"Something got hit," I said.

I later learned that the explosion was really a sonic boom emanating from F-16 fighter jets that had been scrambled from Langley Air Force Base in Hampton, Virginia, some 100 miles from the Pentagon. Trying to reach DC before any of the stray planes hit their targets, the F-16s hit Mach 2—twice the speed of sound, about 1500 miles per hour—creating a rolling acrosonic thunder all the way up Virginia.

A portion of the Pentagon collapsed. A fourth airliner, also hijacked, crashed near Pittsburgh. All of this occurred before 10:22 a.m., when the Justice Department was officially evacuated.

A few men in green military-looking uniforms were shouting from bullhorns to evacuate. I grabbed a handful of mints and some bottles of water and stuffed them in my knapsack. I ducked back in the conference room one last time to check the news and watched with horror as the World Trade Center's north tower melted as if in slow motion, creating another tsunami of dust and debris.

"I'm gone," I said to no one in particular.

On the way home, DC declared a state of emergency. When I finally got to our house, I grasped Dan and the kids and broke down in sobs. I knew I had lost people I cared for and just didn't know about yet. The attack left nearly 3000 dead. Hundreds of first responders to the World Trade Center ruins have since died from illnesses related to their rescue efforts.

After a night of bad dreams about trying to get home, I went back to work the next day for the sake of pretending everything was "business as usual" in the nation's capital. Nothing could have been further from the truth. I started trying to track people down. I stopped after speaking to the crying brother of an old boyfriend, one of over 5000 then missing in New York. People started putting up posters for the missing. Brown University sent an email to all alumni, asking people to reply if they or other alumni they knew were safe. I replied on behalf of myself and Claudia. Military police in green camouflage stood sentry on street corners. Sirens and helicopters blared throughout the day. We were evacuated twice for bomb scares.

I'm still searching, with both the benefit and burden of hindsight, for what caused the breakdown that followed in PRAO and the Justice

Department more broadly. Certainly, government employees at every level of the institutional hierarchy were affected by the events of 9/11 in a very personal way. The Solicitor General's wife, Barbara, was killed aboard the plane that crashed into the Pentagon. A total of 125 people in the Pentagon died—soldiers, civilian employees, and military contractors.

Rosh Hashanah, the Jewish new year, arrived one week later. The liturgy, which I had read for decades, was imbued with new meaning. The opening blessing over the candles could not have been more appropriate: "Grant us this year a glimpse of the light of redemption, the light of healing and of peace."

The rabbi chanted with urgent emphasis in his voice, "Blessed is God for giving us life, for sustaining us, and for enabling us to reach this season." His words gave me chills. An acquaintance of mine had not reached the new season. I just didn't know it yet.

The rabbi intoned: "Grant us peace, your most precious gift. Bless our country, that it may always be a stronghold of peace, and its advocate among the nations." Little did I realize how far we would stray from that prayer as our nation embarked on an indefinite "war on terrorism" and a supposedly short-term attack on the al Qaeda terrorist network and its leader, Osama bin Laden, who eluded our country for another decade.

To the extent that Department attorneys had been risk-averse about the ethical propriety of their conduct—perhaps a bit too much once the McDade Amendment went into effect—after 9/11 it was quite the opposite. People knew no bounds. Anything and everything could and would be done in the name of fighting terrorism.

The cabal of Bush, Vice President Dick Cheney, Ashcroft and Defense Secretary Donald Rumsfeld re-wrote the rules, crushed people, and leveled cities to uproot terrorists and eradicate the problem of Muslim extremists. There was a toxic and intoxicating miasma of moral superiority, machismo, and revenge. The Bush administration's approach also perpetuated a belief that our government couldn't keep us safe within the current confines of due process, privacy, freedoms of speech and association, and checks and balances. In the words of President Bush, "Our nation recognizes that this new paradigm—ushered in not by us, but by terrorists—requires new thinking in the law of war." He didn't tell us that it meant discarding all existing laws of war.

John Yoo, a contemporary of mine from law school, now worked in the rarefied Office of Legal Counsel, which is often considered the "conscience of the Justice Department." That office reviews the most significant and sensitive topics that the federal government considers. As the government's ultimate legal advisor, its memos have the effect of a binding legal opinion on government policy. Assistant Attorney General Jay Bybee headed the office from roughly 2001 to 2003, and Yoo was his deputy. On September 25, Yoo drafted a secret memo to then-White House Counsel Alberto Gonzales (long before Gonzales became famous for politicizing the Justice Department once he became attorney general). It said there were effectively "no limits" on Bush's powers to respond to the attacks of September 11 and that the president's decisions "are for him alone and are unreviewable."

Black September came to a close. Wall Street ended its worst week in sixty-eight years. I got a $3000 raise, which could not have been better timed given the troubled economy and provided reassurance that I was performing well at work. I was grateful when I could concentrate for more than two minutes without my thoughts being interrupted by shards of 9/11.

Jacob, my three-year-old, boggled me with impossible questions: Why did the bad guys make such a mess? Did they catch all of them? Are the bad guys going to do this again? I wanted so badly to reassure him, but did not know the answers. Jacob and his nursery school buddies were constructing Lego towers and knocking them over with pretend airplanes—acting out the unavoidable images that dominated the TV and newspapers.

"Stop it," I snapped. I didn't think I would be on edge for such a sustained period of time. Then I more calmly pleaded, "Please don't do that."

"It's just pretend, Mommy," he said.

"But it's not," I said, realizing the futility of my argument.

When I read him *The Three Little Pigs* that night, he said he was glad our house was made of brick so that the Big Bad Wolf couldn't blow it down. How do you explain terrorism to a child?

At the end of September, DC was slammed by the most destructive tornado to hit the region in seventy-five years. Two University of Maryland students, sisters, were killed. I was disgusted with myself for deriving relief from the fact that it was a natural disaster that caused the loss, not a man-made one.

During the first week in October, the Federal Reserve cut interest rates another half point. It was the ninth cut that year as our country appeared to be sliding into a recession. We had to fly out of town for a family wedding. We were originally routed out of Ronald Reagan Washington National Airport, but it was still closed; so instead we flew from Dulles, which had been used as a launching pad for the terrorist attacks less than a month earlier. For me and a majority of the other passengers, it was our first time flying since 9/11.

The US commenced air strikes against Afghanistan a couple of hours before our return flight, and the news warned of certain and imminent retaliation. Instead of landing, we barely grazed the runway and angled up abruptly like a rocket. Confused looks came over all faces. At that strange moment in time, every passenger had the same thought: We've been hijacked. The cabin was eerily silent. No one was talking. No one was screaming. No one was grabbing for their cell phones. Everyone was waiting. It was the longest two minutes of my life.

Finally, a terse voice emanated over the loudspeaker and explained that we had been forced to do a "touch-and-go" (a procedure developed by the military to squeeze a few more takeoffs and landings into training sessions) to avoid a Northwest Airlines plane in the runway. A hundred passengers sighed with relief. While later waiting in the aisle to exit, we talked about how we were afraid our plane had been turned into a guided missile. On the bus ride back to the terminal, we complained about how long it had taken for the captain to tell us what had really happened. While standing around the baggage carousel, we criticized the air traffic controllers, the airport, our airline, and the other airline.

I was so relieved that we had not been hijacked that it was not until the next day, when a Scandinavian airliner hit a private jet on a runway in Italy killing all aboard, that I realized the magnitude of what had in fact occurred. We were so thankful that we had not been hijacked that no one bothered to thank the pilot for his quick thinking and expert skills that saved us from a deadly collision. It symptomized the aftermath of 9/11: We were so blinded by fear, we could not see the forest through the trees. And the government did everything it could to perpetuate and exacerbate those fears. It is one thing to urge people to be alert; it is another thing to play on their fears in order to accomplish overreaching objectives the country had lived without for more than 200 years.

Castro. Gadaffi. Bin Laden had joined a rogue's gallery of the world's most notorious anti-American megalomaniacs. His propaganda videos kept surfacing on Al Jazeera, the Arab TV network. On the one-month anniversary of the attacks, the president held a prime-time press conference. In a stark warning, the FBI said it had received information that there might be additional terrorist attacks domestically or abroad in the next several days.

Just when I thought the daily stress could get no worse, an anthrax bioterrorist attack began. Letters laced with anthrax created a baffling series of poisonings that touched postal workers, politicians, the news media, and those who were only incidentally exposed through cross-contamination from tainted mail. It started in Florida, where one employee lay dead and seven more exposed; New York had two people similarly affected; and there was a letter in Nevada containing powder that tested positive for anthrax.

Then more anthrax letters surfaced. This time, DC Senate Majority Leader Thomas Daschle's office received one, and the Capitol closed as over thirty people tested positive for anthrax exposure. Two DC postal workers died of pulmonary anthrax and two more became seriously ill with this deadly inhaled form. It was unclear if this bio attack was bin Laden's handiwork or the doings of some unrelated homegrown psychopath. US warplanes were still patrolling over our house throughout the night. The reign of terror had made us scared of our own shadow.

On October 26, 2001, the Justice Department temporarily closed its mail facility in Landover, Maryland. The mail processed at the Landover facility comes directly from the Brentwood facility in DC, where the two postal employees had died. That same morning, President Bush signed the awkwardly titled "Uniting and Strengthening America by Providing Appropriate Tools Required to Intercept and Obstruct Terrorism Act of 2001," better known at the "Patriot Act." It seemed as if Ashcroft started with the acronym and then tried to come up with a name to fit. (It also foreshadowed a number of other liberty-infringing programs and laws dressed in patriotic-sounding names, like the Protect America Act of 2007—a controversial amendment to the Foreign Intelligence Surveillance Act that removed the warrant requirement for the government to spy on Americans.)

The Patriot Act provided for far-reaching changes in federal law enforcement; for example, without a warrant and without probable cause, it gave the FBI new authority to search homes and offices and to monitor phone conversations and email. (No one knew that the National Security Agency was simultaneously taking far more controversial liberties by starting up a secret program to electronically eavesdrop on Americans without warrants.)

A few days later, the Landover facility that processed mail for the Justice Department tested positive for anthrax bacteria. A New Jersey postal worker was found to have pulmonary anthrax, the thirteenth confirmed case since the outbreak began, including five in the DC region. Then we got another terror alert.

Ashcroft seemed to be on TV all the time, usually wearing too much makeup and often with FBI Director Robert Muller III, somberly at his side, offering updates or bleak doomsday warnings. At the end of October, Mueller wrote me a letter thanking me for my article on the McDade Amendment. Frankly, I was surprised he had the time to do so given the obsessive focus on terrorism.

As if it wasn't enough to be worried about anthrax at work, environmental tests found traces of anthrax at our neighborhood post office. This was hitting too close to home, literally. Everyone in DC was stocking up on Cipro and putting crates for mail outside their doors. On Halloween, a New York City hospital worker became the fourth person to die from pulmonary anthrax, which matched the strain of anthrax involved in the other attacks. It was hard to get in the mood for ghosts and goblins. Things were scary enough already. It's only fun when it's make-believe, but the fear was all too real.

November was no better. Osama bin Laden issued another video. We now had warnings of possible terrorist attacks on California bridges. President Bush had an eighty-six percent approval rating and Ashcroft's hovered near seventy percent. Fear proved great for political ratings. I felt like our country was suffering from a collective post-traumatic stress disorder, which included symptoms of isolation, hyper-vigilance, and severe anxiety. How else to account for the political and legal excesses in the aftermath of 9/11? None of us were behaving rationally. Then by chance, I became involved in a pivotal event that exemplified this new hysteria.

# "AMERICAN TALIBAN"

J OHN WALKER, eventually identified by his full name, John Walker Lindh, converted to Islam when he was sixteen years old. He embarked on a spiritual quest to Yemen in 2000 to study classical Arabic and Islamic theology. By the spring of 2001, however, he became convinced that it was incumbent upon devout Muslims to do more than just read and pray. He felt called to train for military *jihad*. In June 2001, he crossed the border into Afghanistan to volunteer for the Afghan army, which was engaged in a protracted civil war between the now-deposed Taliban government and the Northern Alliance. His father later likened him to Ernest Hemingway during the Spanish Civil War—he had volunteered for the army of a foreign government battling an insurgency. While the Hemingway allusion may be inapt, Lindh viewed the Taliban, the *de facto* government of Afghanistan, as upholders of Islam.

The United States' aid to the Taliban dated back to the Soviet invasion of Afghanistan, when the Taliban served as anticommunist opposition. During the Carter administration, the Reagan administration, the first Bush administration, the Clinton administration, and the second Bush administration, the US provided the Taliban army with military and humanitarian assistance. In fact, four months before 9/11, the US government gave $43 million in humanitarian aid to Afghanistan. Meanwhile, the Russian government continued to fund the brutal Northern Alliance up until 2001, the year Lindh joined the Afghan resistance movement. In his own words, Lindh "saw the war between the Taliban and the Northern Alliance as a continuation of the war between the *mujahedeen* and the Soviets" and wanted to be one of the freedom fighters.

In Lindh's naïve view, he was just protecting Afghan civilian Muslims from savage attacks by the Northern Alliance warlords who were trying to overthrow the Taliban government. He wanted to be a soldier for the Islamic liberation movement against the warlords who controlled northern Afghanistan provinces and were subjugating ordinary citizens. In joining an Islamic paramilitary program run by a Pakistani organization that trained Muslims to fight against Indian security forces, he did not have a sophisticated understanding of the complex conflict between Pakistan and India over the disputed territory of Kashmir. Nor did he know that the Taliban had an atrocious human rights record.

Because of his language deficiencies, Taliban recruiters made Lindh join al-Ansar, which put him in a training camp called al-Farooq, where there were two kinds of courses: 1) al Qaeda training to fight the Northern Alliance; and 2) very basic military training that entailed spending eighteen hours a day praying, exercising, eating, attending classes on weapons and warfare, and performing routine chores.

A week before September 11, Lindh finally arrived on the Taliban's front line, where he performed sentry duty, which entailed a lot of downtime for reading. He did not know that after September 11, the Bush administration became hostile to the Taliban and cut off support. Nor did he know that his home country would soon view him as the traitor incarnate. Never could I have imagined that the government would view me the same way.

The United States began bombing Afghan targets in October and started hitting Lindh's post by November 5. By November 10, his unit was in a panicked retreat to Kunduz. They fled fifty miles on foot over unforgiving desert terrain. Over a treacherous two days, they lost a third of their men. On November 21, the regional Taliban military leader negotiated a surrender of the unit with the notoriously savage General Dostum of the Northern Alliance, who was a former Soviet collaborator-turned-warlord. Lindh's commander had agreed to pay Dostum in exchange for safe passage across Northern Alliance territory to the Taliban stronghold of Herat. From there, Lindh planned to escape to Pakistan and return home.

But Lindh's commander was double-crossed. The cash was paid, but the Northern Alliance took the Taliban soldiers prisoner and detained them at Qala-i-Jangi, an ancient fortress on the outskirts of Mazar-i-Sharif in northern Afghanistan that was serving as the military headquarters of Dostum. When a Taliban prisoner resisted, Northern Alliance guards herded the 400 prisoners into the basement of a sturdy Soviet-built schoolhouse. Dostum's men dropped a grenade down an air duct, which narrowly missed Lindh but wounded and killed several of his fellow captives. As memorialized in video footage, on November 25, the prisoners were led out of the basement into the courtyard of the old fortress, forced to kneel in rows, and kicked and beaten with sticks. Lindh was knocked in the head and nearly lost consciousness. The Northern Alliance and two armed CIA officers, Johnny "Mike" Spann and Dave Tyson, circulated among the prisoners.

They singled out Lindh and separated him from the group for questioning. Without identifying himself as an agent of the US government, Spann threatened Lindh with death.

"You believe in what you're doing here that much, you're willing to be killed here?" Spann asked in a video that was seen by millions in the days following Lindh's capture.

"He's got to decide if he wants to live or die, and die here," Tyson told Spann, within earshot of Lindh. "We're just going to leave him, and he's going to fucking sit in prison the rest of his fucking short life. It's his decision."

Lindh did not respond and was returned to the larger group of prisoners.

Suddenly an explosion and shouting signaled a spontaneous uprising. The Northern Alliance troops reacted by shooting scores of bound, unarmed prisoners, many of whom died with their arms still tied behind their backs. The grisly revolt, in which Lindh was not a participant, led to Lindh's getting shot in the right thigh by an AK-47 bullet and to Spann's death—the first American to die in combat in the war in Afghanistan.

Though neither man caused the other's injury, Lindh would later be charged with conspiracy to commit murder in the death of Spann. Even though the judge eventually found that "[t]he government has no evidence of that," the government would still bring Spann's parents and widow to the courthouse and stage an emotional press conference in which the Spann family denounced Lindh as a traitor and demanded that he be given the death penalty.

Lindh played dead for a day before Taliban soldiers helped him and other wounded survivors into the basement of a building in a fortress, where they would spend the next six harrowing days. The Northern Alliance tried to flush out the unarmed, wounded, starving prisoners with gunfire, hand grenades, and ignited diesel fuel. Finally, the Northern Alliance flooded the basement with freezing water, which quickly became polluted with blood, human waste, and floating body parts.

Miraculously, Lindh and eighty-five others survived, and he was taken into military custody on December 1. According to a secret document I obtained from a journalist in June 2004, an Army intelligence officer "advised that before interviewing Lindh, instructions came from higher headquarters for him to coordinate with JSOTF [the Joint Special Operations Task Force] JAG officer. He was told . . . he could collect on anything criminal that was volunteered."

But Higher Headquarters told the intelligence officer more than that. Rumsfeld's office told him not to handle Lindh with kid gloves. In a stunning revelation, the document states: "The Admiral told him that the Secretary of Defense's counsel [William Haynes II] had authorized him to 'take the gloves off' and ask whatever he wanted." These instructions to get tough with Lindh are the earliest known evidence that the Bush administration was willing to push the envelope on how far it could go to extract information from suspected terrorists.

In a reversal of the usual legal procedure, according to this document, the "JAG had said that if Lindh said anything incriminating, read him his rights." Needless to say, it defeats the purpose of reading someone their Miranda rights only after they have already made incriminating statements. The purpose of the Miranda warning, which most Americans can recite more accurately than the words to *America, the Beautiful*, is to neutralize the distinct psychological disadvantage that suspects are under when dealing with interrogators. After a person has been taken into custody, but before any interrogation takes place, the subject must be Mirandized. The Army intelligence officer "told the JAG he did not have a copy of Miranda and asked JSOTF to send Miranda by fax but he never got it. He never gave Lindh the Miranda warnings."

US Special Forces interrogated Lindh and tied his hands with rope, pulled a hood over his head, drove him for several hours, placed him in a dark room, and called him vulgar names. Lindh repeatedly requested counsel, but met with indifference.

*Newsweek* first broke the story, dubbing Lindh the "American Taliban." That night, Lindh's mother, Marilyn Walker, found an MSNBC article describing a young American who had been found among a group of Taliban prisoners of war in northern Afghanistan. He said he was twenty years old, had been born in Washington, DC, was an American citizen, and had converted to Islam. She called her ex-husband, Frank Lindh.

By the next morning, Marilyn Walker had spoken with the State Department, the ACLU, Amnesty International, and Human Rights Watch, and all had flatly declined to provide assistance. As Frank Lindh later explained:

> This was an especially painful moment for us. It appeared that John's case was so controversial, his cause so hopeless, that nobody would be willing to come to his defense. John was wounded and had nearly been killed under incredible circumstances on the other side of the world. As his parents, we felt desperate for help.

Frank Lindh then called legendary trial lawyer James Brosnahan, who agreed to meet him the next morning, December 3.

The public attention created nothing short of mass hysteria. By the time Brosnahan and Frank Lindh met, virtually every American newspaper was running front-page stories about the "American Taliban," every radio show was discussing him, and images of him were constantly shown on TV. President Bush initially seemed somewhat sympathetic, telling a TV reporter, "Obviously he has, uh, been misled, it appears to me, and thought he was going to fight for a great cause, and in fact, he was going to support a government that was one of the most repressive governments in the history of mankind."

But soon Bush, Cheney, Rumsfeld, Secretary of State Colin Powell, and Senators Hillary Clinton and John McCain made inflammatory comments and prejudicial statements that Lindh was an al Qaeda fighter, terrorist, and traitor; had fired his weapon; had attended a terrorist training camp; and had foreknowledge of 9/11—even though the government from the first day of Lindh's capture was in possession of facts to the contrary. Attorney General Ashcroft even said that Lindh had been led personally by Osama bin Laden: "He chose to embrace fanatics, and his allegiance to those terrorists never faltered."

Lindh's parents tried to write to him through the International Red Cross, but were informed that the US military authorities would not allow their letters through. The military authorities also refused the Red Cross's request to visit Lindh to check on his condition. Lindh would become the first American to be prosecuted as part of the Bush administration's war on terrorism.

# THE CALL

S HORTLY AFTER MEETING with Frank Lindh, Brosnahan faxed
a letter to a number of key government officials, including
Powell, Ashcroft, Rumsfeld, CIA Director George Tenet, and
CIA General Counsel Robert McNamara, Jr. The letter informed
them that Brosnahan had been hired by Lindh's parents to represent
their son and asked that any further interrogation of him be halted.

On December 7, Lindh was flown to Camp Rhino, a US Marine
base in the high Afghan desert south of Kandahar, a former stronghold of the Taliban regime. He was blindfolded, stripped naked,
bound to a board with duct tape, taunted, threatened, and locked
in an unheated and unlit metal shipping container that sat on an
ice cold floor. That day, on what I thought would be a laid back
Friday, I received a call from John De Pue, a counterterrorism
prosecutor in the Criminal Division's Terrorism and Violent Crime
Section.

"The FBI wants to interview 'American Taliban' member John
Walker [Lindh] sometime next week," De Pue informed me. "The
interview would occur in Afghanistan. [His] father retained counsel

for him and the FBI wants to question [him] about taking up arms against the US."

This type of situation (contact with a represented person) formed the bulk of the inquiries at PRAO because the ethics rules prohibit communication with people represented by counsel. We were told unambiguously that Lindh had counsel. In the advice we later rendered, the premise that Lindh had counsel was never questioned. We never suggested for a minute an argument that this American was somehow not "really" represented—the argument that the Justice Department ultimately put forth.

I consulted with Claudia and a senior legal advisor, Joan Goldfrank. Our office, as was the case with many other offices at Justice, had been abuzz all week with the shocking news of the "American Taliban." The American people, still reeling from 9/11, were clearly out for blood. You could feel the hunger for a modern-day legal lynching, a term used for historic show trials of black men in death penalty cases. But this time the lynching would make an example of a Muslim American in a terrorism case.

What jurisdiction would he be tried in? Virginia was the most conservative, compared to California—a logical venue because that is where he was from. Was there any way to charge him with treason? It was one of the only offenses punishable by death. Had he killed CIA Agent Mike Spann during the uprising at Mazar-i-Sharif? Spann had interrogated Lindh for about thirty minutes before the start of the uprising.

The Department of Justice and the public at large had it in for Lindh. The hue and cry was deafening.

I responded that interviewing Lindh would not be authorized by law under the ethics rules. The specific rule that governs contact by a lawyer with a person represented by counsel is set forth in the American Bar Association (ABA) Rule of Professional Conduct 4.2, the "anti-contact rule," which was the Achilles' heel of prosecutors. It states that "[i]n representing a client, a lawyer shall not communicate about the subject of the representation with a person the lawyer knows to be represented by another lawyer in the matter, unless the lawyer has the consent of the other lawyer or is authorized to do so by law or a court order." The rule expressly provides for *ex parte* communications (without the consent of the represented person's lawyer) that are "authorized by law."

The majority of circuit courts, including those in which Lindh could be indicted, had held that covert (undercover), pre-indictment, non-custodial contacts with represented persons during criminal investigations do not violate the rule. For example, it would be okay for an undercover agent or confidential informant to contact a represented person who had not been arrested or formally charged. But Lindh's situation struck out on two of those three criteria. He was in custody and his interview would be overt—therefore contact was not authorized by law.

However, my colleagues and I still tried to think of some creative ways that the FBI could interview the "American Taliban" and stay within ethical boundaries; for example, I suggested that since his parents were saying publicly that they thought their son was brainwashed, the FBI could ask Lindh if he really wanted an attorney of their choosing.

By the end of the day, US officials released a list of six possible charges, including treason, murder, and conspiracy, that Lindh could face. Most carried a possible death sentence upon conviction.

On December 9 at Camp Rhino, after two days in the steel shipping container, Lindh was removed. FBI Agent Christopher Reimann began extracting the confession from Lindh that became the basis for the eventual and ill-advised criminal case. Reimann read Lindh the Miranda warning, but admits that when noting the right to counsel, he ad-libbed, "Of course, there are no lawyers here." Lindh was not told that his parents had retained an attorney for him who was willing to fly to Afghanistan. Worried that he would be returned to the container, which in fact happened at the conclusion of the two-day interrogation, Lindh signed a waiver, which was improperly administered and clearly raised voluntariness issues.

On Monday, De Pue called again with news from the Deputy Legal Advisor of the FBI: Despite our advice not to question Lindh without counsel, an agent interviewed him over the weekend. De Pue wanted to know what to do now.

I was surprised, but not shocked, that our advice was disregarded, because the FBI had a reputation for being a bunch of cowboys who did their own thing. What really surprised me was that the Criminal Division was so quick to confess error and that they actually wanted to know how to correct it—something our office was also used to doing.

"The interview may have to be sealed and used only for national security purposes or intelligence gathering," I explained, "not for criminal prosecution. But I need more information."

Meanwhile, Claudia told me to pull all the advice our office had ever issued in cases of "unauthorized contacts" (unethical contacts with a person represented by counsel), recognizing this for exactly what it was. We were in crisis-management mode.

During the following five days, Lindh was placed on board a US naval ship, the *USS Peleliu*, and two weeks after he had been transferred to American military custody, Navy physicians finally removed the bullet from his leg. Meanwhile, I followed up repeatedly with De Pue because he was the one who had initiated both of the contacts with our office. Claudia soon told me, "Our office's involvement in this matter is over."

This abrupt termination was unprecedented when our office's advice had been so flagrantly ignored; our mission was not only to keep attorneys out of trouble, but also to help them correct the matter if mistakes had been made. Usually, there was a way to do so—by implementing screening mechanisms, such as sealing off a questionable interview and creating a "taint team," or by seeking a court's guidance. But in this case, Claudia told me to close the file two weeks after opening it. De Pue seemed just as eager to end our communiqués.

It wasn't long before I learned why.

In January 2002, the Justice Department issued a series of memoranda, many of them authored by the Office of Legal Counsel (the same office that wrote the Patriot Act), which read more like immunization documents, to keep US officials from being charged with crimes for the way prisoners were detained and interrogated.

The memos, especially one written on January 9 to Haynes, the general counsel of the Defense Department, addressed "the effect of international treaties and federal laws on the treatment of individuals detained by the US Armed Forces during the conflict in Afghanistan." It failed to analyze two critical sources of law: a treaty (the Convention Against Torture) and a federal law (the Anti-Torture Statute). Instead, it provided legal arguments to support administration officials' assertions that the Geneva Conventions did not apply to the detainees from the war in Afghanistan—namely, any member of the Taliban or al Qaeda. And John Walker Lindh was detainee 001.

William Taft IV, great-grandson of President Taft, had served in Haynes's position from 1981 to 1984. Now the State Department's top legal advisor and the government's principal interpreter of treaties, Taft wrote a blunt letter to Yoo on January 11, 2002. It dispensed with the usual bureaucratic niceties and excoriated Justice's legal advice to President Bush about detainees as "legally flawed and procedurally impossible," its reasoning as "incorrect and incomplete," and its arguments as "contrary to the official position of the United States, the United Nations, and all other states that have considered the issue."

Less than a month after I closed the Lindh file, Ashcroft announced the filing of criminal charges against Lindh—something I had advised against. Although the government's own evidence showed that Lindh had done nothing more than volunteer as a foot soldier in the Afghan army, Ashcroft began his dramatic televised statement by referring to 9/11 and saying, "We cannot overlook the attacks on America when they come from United States citizens." He claimed that Lindh had "knowingly and purposely allied himself with certain terrorist organizations," and that he had "embraced" those who "had murdered thousands of his countrymen." The statement violated Justice Department guidelines on the release of information related to criminal proceedings, which are intended to ensure that a defendant is not prejudiced by pre-trial publicity.

A reporter stood up. "Sir, even though he was Mirandized, his family has complained several times that they haven't had the chance to get his lawyer in to talk to him yet. Do you know how soon his lawyer will have access to him now that these charges have been filed?"

"Well, I think it's important to understand that the subject here is entitled to choose his own lawyer," the attorney general explained, "and to our knowledge, has not chosen a lawyer at this time."

In an about-face from the operative facts with which I was provided—that Lindh was represented by counsel—Ashcroft appeared to be saying that the lawyer whom Lindh's father had hired to represent him was not legitimate because Lindh had not personally retained him. What Ashcroft neglected to mention was that the lawyer had sent letters to him, Rumsfeld, Powell, Tenet, and McNamara informing them that he represented Lindh and wanted to meet with his client, and that those efforts were deliberately blocked. For more than fifty days after receiving Brosnahan's letter, the government continued to hold and interrogate Lindh without giving him access to legal counsel and without telling him his family had retained a lawyer to represent him.

The day after the unorthodox press conference, the first suspected al Qaeda and Taliban prisoners began arriving at the new-fangled US prison camp on Guantánamo Bay Naval Base (abbreviated as GTMO, pronounced "Gitmo") in Cuba, which presumably would have been John Walker Lindh's fate if he had not been a US citizen. Gitmo was a transparent attempt to hold these detainees away from federal court review.

Based on the advice of White House and Justice Department lawyers, on January 18, President Bush decided that the Geneva Conventions would not apply to members of al Qaeda and the Taliban, and Rumsfeld sent a memo to that effect to the chairman of the US Joint Chiefs of Staff (the military's most senior leaders.)

Unbeknownst to me, on January 22, Claudia faxed three of my emails about Lindh to Ken Melson, the Criminal Chief of the US Attorney's Office for the Eastern District of Virginia, which had jurisdiction over Lindh and the majority of other terrorism cases that the government would later bring. That same day, the Justice Department sent a thirty-seven-page memo, authored by Bybee, to the White House and Pentagon, which argued that the War Crimes Act and the Geneva Conventions did not apply to al Qaeda prisoners and that President Bush had constitutional authority to "suspend our treaty obligations toward Afghanistan" because it was a "failed state."

Lindh arrived back in the United States on January 23, chained up in a military plane. He was sent to the Alexandria city jail in Virginia, where his parents tried to visit him but were turned away.

The next morning, Lindh had his first court appearance, where he met his lawyer for the first time in a brief, ten-minute conference before his preliminary hearing. Judge T. S. Ellis III, set a trial date for late August, which meant that Lindh would be on trial just a few miles from the Pentagon on the one-year anniversary of 9/11. The defense team was deeply troubled by the timing, especially in light of Ashcroft's intemperate remarks.

On January 25, White House Counsel Gonzales wrote a memo to President Bush concluding that the Justice Department's advice in the January 9 memo was sound and that the president should declare the Taliban and al Qaeda outside the protections of the Geneva Conventions because the war on terrorism "renders obsolete Geneva's strict limitations on the questioning of enemy prisoners and renders quaint some of its provisions." No one in their wildest dreams foresaw the frightening potential of the next president prosecuting US citizens under the Espionage Act, thus making them not merely enemy prisoners, but also enemies of the state.

The next day, Secretary of State Powell wrote a memo to Gonzales at the White House, making clear that the advantages of applying the Geneva Conventions far outweighed their rejection. Powell's swift dissent argued that declaring the conventions inapplicable would "reverse over a century of US policy and practice in supporting the Geneva Conventions and undermine the protections of the law of war for our troops, both in this specific conflict and in general." He also said, with great foresight, that it would "undermine public support among critical allies."

The following day, Secretary Rumsfeld made his first visit to Guantánamo Bay and declared that the prisoners there "will not be determined to be POWs," summarily removing them from a panoply of protections.

At our weekly staff meeting on January 29, Claudia announced that our office had been taking a more conservative position lately. That was an understatement. That same day, President Bush said the detainees at Guantánamo would not be treated as prisoners of war, though their exact legal status was still being "worked out." It is still being worked out ten years later.

On February 1, 2002, Ashcroft sent Bush a twelve-paragraph memo warning in stark terms (as Ashcroft was inclined to do) that if the president sided with the State Department's reading of the Geneva Conventions, American officials might wind up going to jail for violating US and international laws—a tacit admission that they were. Ashcroft's memo should have raised red flags.

Taft, on behalf of the State Department, wrote a memo the next day to the White House, reiterating Powell's warning that the broad rejection of the Geneva Conventions could put US troops at risk if they were captured now or in future conflicts. The State Department memo also advised that following Geneva standards "demonstrates that the United States bases its conduct not just on its policy preferences, but on its international legal obligations." An attachment to the memo noted that CIA lawyers asked for an explicit understanding that their operatives were exempt from the administration's public pledge to abide by the spirit of the Geneva Conventions. The issue of liability continued to plague the government into the next presidential administration, when President Barack Obama—a majority of the electorate's great hope for accountability—decided early in his term not to prosecute CIA operatives who used interrogation practices described by many as torture.

On February 4, Claudia strode into my office as if she were on a mission, closed the door behind her, and handed me a performance evaluation. It was not the usual time for evaluations, and it was not as if they were just being distributed to everyone late. No one else received one. Curiously, it was unsigned. It also covered a nine-month rating period (the usual was three months) that had ended four months earlier.

"I know what's in here will come as a shock to you," she warned, "but you just don't seem happy working here."

I conceded that I wasn't happy with my colleague Joan Goldfrank's triviality and jealousy in the aftermath of my *Georgetown* article and amity with Larry Thompson, but that I loved legal ethics.

"Well, I think you need to find a new job. Otherwise, I'll have to put this evaluation in your permanent personnel file."

This seemed like an extreme edict, but I had not yet read the evaluation. When I did so, it was beyond blistering. It was downright cruel. I started crying because no one had ever said such vicious things about me. Moreover, it was filled with blatant lies. For example, it said:

> In one matter, she drafted a motion for an AUSA in which she failed to present a routine legal issue . . . in a correct, coherent fashion . . . [It] was deficient in its organization, in the arguments it presented and in its rendition of the issues and the legal authorities.

The assistant US attorney with whom I had drafted the motion, David Cortes, had chosen to submit the motion we drafted together instead of the weak revision drafted by one of my supervisors. The motion was granted, and the judge published an opinion, which was based verbatim on the motion. The opinion was later cited favorably in the ABA's *Annotated Model Rules of Professional Conduct,* our office's legal ethics bible.

The telling line in the performance evaluation, however, excoriated me for being, essentially, too uppity: "She took inappropriate actions that indicated that she did not understand her role in the office viz-à-viz higher level officials." In other words, by accepting Larry Thompson's lunch invitation, I had stepped out of my place.

That seemed so petty, but the theme was repeated throughout the vituperative evaluation:

> With respect to understanding her position in the office . . . Ms. Radack contacted a senior official in the office of the Deputy Attorney General without the knowledge or approval of anyone in PRAO, including the Director [Claudia Flynn] who reports directly to the official in question. These communications manifest a serious lapse in judgment by Ms. Radack.

It appeared that my friendship with Larry had bent some noses out of joint.

The evaluation was so over the top—and contradicted by my professional track record (a merit bonus less than a year earlier, a groundbreaking published judicial opinion based on a brief I wrote, a law review article in a prestigious academic journal, a raise, and recognition from senior agency heads)—that it was clear something else was going on. I just didn't yet know or understand what.

Claudia's threat that the vitriolic missive would be placed in my personnel file if I did not leave was something I took seriously because I planned on being a career civil servant and relied on my unblemished academic and employment record toward that end.

The very next day, Ashcroft held a press conference and demagogically announced Lindh's formal indictment. "John Walker Lindh chose to train with al Qaeda, chose to fight with the Taliban, chose to be led by Osama bin Laden," Ashcroft stated. "[T]he fact of those choices is clear. Americans who love their country do not dedicate themselves to killing Americans." Even William F. Buckley's conservative *National Review* criticized Ashcroft's prejudicial statements about a pending prosecution as "inappropriate" and "gratuitous."

In an audacious and unflinching statement, Ashcroft claimed with a straight face, "At each step in this process, Walker Lindh's rights . . . have been carefully, scrupulously honored." I knew Ashcroft was lying, but I still did not put two and two together.

# A FATEFUL CHOICE

O N February 7, 2002, Bybee advised Gonzales that the president had "reasonable factual grounds" to determine that Taliban fighters captured in Afghanistan were not entitled to POW status.

There was a seemingly irresolvable schism, with State Department officials and military lawyers on one side and the White House, Justice Department, and Defense Department on the other. Later that day, President Bush issued a directive that settled the scorched-earth memos battle in favor of the Justice Department: The Geneva Conventions would apply to Taliban prisoners, but not to al Qaeda prisoners. Bush said that he believed he had "the authority under the Constitution" to deny protections of the Geneva Conventions to combatants picked up during the war in Afghanistan, but that he would "decline to exercise that authority at this time." In one of his many mixed messages, he simultaneously declared that all Taliban detainees were "unlawful combatants" who were not entitled to POW status.

The criminal case against Lindh continued to proceed at lightning speed in the Eastern District of Virginia, known as the "rocket docket" for its precision-like disposition of important cases. On February 15, Judge Ellis, who was presiding over the Lindh case, issued a discovery order. In essence, it ordered that all copies of the Justice Department's internal correspondence about the conditions of Lindh's interrogation be sent to him so that he could determine if the documents should be passed on to the defense team. Claudia concealed the order from me.

A week later, again without telling me that she was circulating my emails to senior Department officials, Claudia faxed to Alice Fisher, the deputy assistant attorney general of the Criminal Division, the same three emails she had faxed a month earlier to Ken Melson, the US attorney for the district in which Lindh was being prosecuted. On February 26, Bybee sent a memo from the Justice Department to the Pentagon's general counsel, Haynes, arguing that the constitutional protections against self-incrimination do not apply to detainees at Guantánamo Bay because they are not being tried in US criminal courts.

In March 2002, the CIA established a secret prison in Thailand to house Abu Zubaydah, the first major al Qaeda target captured. (The US government now admits that he was never a member of al Qaeda, nor involved in the attacks on 9/11, but he is still in custody.) The public did not learn about the CIA's "black sites" until November 2005, when news broke that the CIA maintains its own network of secret prisons into which 100 or more terrorist suspects have "disappeared," as if victims of a Third World dictatorship. Two secret CIA prisons operated in Poland and Romania until they were shut down following a Human Rights Watch report of their existence. Another CIA prison operated in the North African desert.

March 7, 2002, was the pivotal day for me, when two and two finally added up to four. I got to work to find an email from Assistant US Attorney Randy Bellows, the lead prosecutor in the Lindh case.

He informed me that he had filed two of the emails between De Pue and me with the court, but wanted confirmation that he had all Lindh-related communications I had written so that he could comply with the court's discovery order. I wondered, *What discovery order?* His contact was the first time I'd heard that there was a discovery order in the Lindh case. Even though such orders are normally distributed far and wide at Justice, no one within PRAO had advised me of the court's order or asked me to assist with compliance, even though I was the author and most likely source at PRAO of the materials sought by the court. Additionally, I had written far more than two emails.

Why was Bellows contacting me, a line attorney, directly? A number of people suggested to me that Bellows was doing due diligence because he was keenly aware of Justice Department discovery violations from his work as the head of the Attorney General's Review Team, which submitted a 778-page internal report in May of 2000 that was eventually made part of Congressional oversight hearings. It investigated the FBI's bungling of the Wen Ho Lee case and discussed, for example, how during the trial of Oklahoma City bomber Timothy McVeigh, the Justice Department and the FBI failed to turn over to the defense more than 4400 pages of FBI documents on the case. This error forced Ashcroft to stay McVeigh's execution for a month. It seemed that Bellows didn't want to get similarly burned.

I was concerned immediately because I knew there were many more emails than the couple Bellows possessed. I didn't think anything suspect was going on—just that there had been some kind of major bureaucratic error and that it needed to be corrected as soon as possible. Claudia wasn't in yet, so I forwarded Bellows's email to her and emphasized that there were more emails generated by our office than the two that he had.

Claudia came in shortly afterward and I rushed to tell her about this discrepancy. She got very defensive. Staring daggers at me, she whispered in a slow, deliberate voice, "I sent *everything* that was in the file."

This was news to me. It was the first I leaned that my emails had been sent to anyone besides John De Pue, my original correspondent. I told Claudia that I knew of substantially more relevant emails than the two that Bellows possessed.

Still in naïve mode, I went and checked the hard copy file, which had been an inch-thick stack of paper bound by a heavy-duty, long-reach staple. I felt sick as soon as I saw what was—and what was not—inside. A fist-sized knot formed in my stomach. The file contained only three emails—very innocuous ones. The three that were in there did not even seem logical. There was our initial advice but nothing from the we-ignored-your-advice-and-did-it-anyway aftermath. There was a reply from De Pue, but not the underlying message from me. And there was the final email saying that Lindh had been Mirandized and therefore De Pue was closing out the file on his end. I had submitted more than a dozen emails for the file, all of which I had personally stapled to the "Inquiry Data Sheet," which ensures that documents are properly filed.

I was alarmed because whatever had transpired seemed so deliberate. Claudia was the last person to have handled the file, as evidenced by the fax cover sheets. Her handwriting was literally all over the two fax cover sheets indicating that she sent the three surviving emails to Ken Melson and Alice Fisher.

I immediately confided in Donald Mackay, a trusted and seasoned colleague on the verge of retirement, who had served six years as the US attorney for the Southern District of Illinois. He examined the file and said very matter-of-factly, "This file has been purged."

I couldn't believe my ears. I had never heard that expression—"purged"—used in the context of a government file. The word conjured up bulimic adolescent girls, not high-level government officials. Besides, it was just inconceivable. At that time, the Department of Justice was pursuing accounting giant Arthur Anderson for obstruction of justice and destruction of evidence related to the Enron investigation. How was this any different?

I was confronted with an unmistakable intimation to overlook violations of law. My new understanding imposed unpalatable choices between the threat of discipline for perceived insubordination (for which Claudia had already evidenced her propensity), or potential liability for knowingly breaking government ethics rules, and possibly the law, by remaining a silent observer who passively acquiesces to betrayals of the law and the public trust.

I called my husband Dan and explained the court order I was not told about and the missing emails. "I don't know exactly what is going on here, but I don't want to be part of it. I'm going to resign. Can you see on your end how close you are to having your contract converted to a permanent position?"

Then I went to Don. "What should I do?" I asked, feeling even more anxious.

"You need to cover your ass, that's what," he said, not mincing words. "Call the computer help line, retrieve as many of those emails as you can, write a memo to Claudia, and staple all the missing emails to it."

I called technical support. The woman with whom I spoke explained that even though I had "deleted" the emails and emptied my virtual "trash" months earlier, the emails could still be retrieved from the hard drive. Rarely does anything *really* disappear, a difficult concept for digital-era newbies to grasp. The computer wizard walked me through a number of ballet steps to retrieve the emails from electronic storage, though to this day, I still don't know if I was able to recover all of them.

As Don recommended, I wrote a memo to Claudia that referenced the two emails from me to De Pue, which Bellows possessed. The

49

memo listed the three emails that survived in the PRAO file. I then listed, and attached copies of, fourteen additional emails missing from the PRAO file that I had been able to resurrect from my computer. Finally, the memo asked Claudia to let me know if she wanted me to send Bellows the emails he did not have. I made a copy of the memo in case the emails "disappeared" again, and I placed the original on her chair because she was not in her office.

I encountered Claudia on the elevator a couple of hours later. "Why weren't those emails in the file?" she snapped. It seemed like a rhetorical question.

I told her I had no idea. In my mind I was countering, You *tell me, Claudia. Why* weren't *those emails in the file?*

"Now I have to explain why PRAO shouldn't look bad for not turning them over," she barked, exasperated. I found her comment odd because I thought her primary concern, like mine, would be to ensure that the missing emails made it to the court as soon as possible.

"Do you want me to send them to Bellows?" I asked.

"No," she said firmly, "*I'll* handle it."

"I'll be tendering my resignation," I stated, and walked out.

She never followed up with me about whether the emails were turned over to Bellows or to the court. When I asked, she just glared at me. From contemporaneous and subsequent public statements made by the Justice Department, it did not sound as if they were.

During the next few weeks, Claudia came by my office as if nothing had happened, acting very solicitous and giving me job leads in other sections of the Justice Department and other government agencies. I wondered why she would do that if she thought I was such a screw-up, but she clearly wanted me gone.

The newspapers were filled with articles about the "American Taliban." The loaded label dehumanized him and turned him into something "other," an "other" that was bad and dangerous. The media and legal scholars were all in agreement about one thing: The main legal issue in the case turned on whether the confession Lindh made to FBI interrogators in Afghanistan should be admissible at trial.

A grand jury relied heavily on Lindh's statements when charging him with conspiring to kill Americans abroad and providing assistance to terrorist groups, including Osama bin Laden's al Qaeda network. If convicted, Lindh could face life in prison. My emails contained information about the interrogation during which Lindh had made the most incriminating statements. The defense was seeking the emails, and I was not at all confident that the Justice Department had ever turned them over; in fact, I was quite certain that it had not.

On March 22, 2002, to the relief of both of us, my husband obtained a permanent job with the World Bank after being a consultant for a number of years. The position provided health insurance for our entire family, which allowed me to quit without leaving us in a medical lurch.

Claudia threw me a big going-away party and gave me a plaque thanking me for my distinguished service to the country. But I left the Justice Department feeling sickened by the apparent cover-up in which I was an unwitting participant.

When I first tried to surmise the motivation for the cover-up, I thought that maybe Claudia was trying to protect the FBI, which by all accounts had been aggressive in its handling of Lindh. There was the haunting photo that went out around the world. It was public that Lindh was left injured, starving, freezing, and sleep-deprived in a pitch-dark steel shipping container. So the missing emails, which documented the FBI's disregarding our ethics advice and looking like a bunch of thugs, wouldn't have helped dispel this image.

But I later gained a more nuanced understanding of the cover-up. I came to see that our office's advice, and my emails in particular, directly contradicted the public position ultimately taken by the attorney general, and someone wanted to hide that PRAO had ever taken a contrary stance—namely, that Lindh was represented by counsel, could not be interrogated without his lawyer, and therefore the subsequent interrogation was unethical and could not be used against him in a criminal prosecution. Someone in the management chain of command, acting either alone or in concert with others, sanitized the file. That person or persons hoped to avoid detection of their duplicity by forcing me from the Department and trying to discredit me.

On April 8, 2002, within a month of discovering the cover-up, I started a new job at Hawkins, Delafield & Wood, a private law firm where I practiced affordable housing law, an area completely unrelated to my expertise and former position. This new job offered me a quick exit from an impossible work situation, the opportunity to do socially redeeming work, and a twenty-five percent salary increase to boot.

In May, the Lindh case was constantly in the news. There was no escaping it. And every journalist in print, radio, and television seemed to be reading off the Justice Department script as the government released a steady stream of false, misleading, and highly inflammatory propaganda to the media. While getting dressed early one morning in June, I heard a broadcast on our local affiliate of National Public Radio stating that the Justice Department had "never" taken the position that Lindh was entitled to counsel, a sentiment that I had heard expressed repeatedly during the preceding weeks and months. I knew this statement was not true. This assertion also indicated to me that the Justice Department had not turned over my emails to the court pursuant to the discovery order. I did not believe that the Department would have the temerity to make public statements contradicted by its own court filings if the emails had indeed been provided. This knowledge weighed heavily on me and turned me into a raging insomniac.

I decided to blow the whistle. My decision came before whistle-blowing enjoyed a brief celebration, courtesy of *TIME Magazine*'s 2002

"Persons of the Year." I was aware of the Whistleblower Protection Act because, ironically, I wrote a memo on it when I worked at PRAO. The Act provides protection to federal government employees who expose government fraud, waste, and abuse. It prohibits an agency official from taking an adverse personnel action against a former or current employee as a reprisal for any disclosure of information by an employee that the employee reasonably believes evidences a violation of any law, rule, or regulation; gross mismanagement; or an abuse of authority. The situation I found myself in couldn't be a more fitting example.

The language of the whistleblower law contemplates a disclosure to anyone inside or outside the agency in which the whistleblower is or was employed, including a reporter, a member of Congress, or an interest group representative. This interpretation is well supported by case law. Interestingly—and somewhat counterintuitively (because the logical place most employees would begin to report a problem is to their supervisors)—the US Court of Appeals for the Federal Circuit held that complaints to a supervisor about the supervisor's own conduct are *not* disclosures covered by the Whistleblower Protection Act; thus, reporting misconduct up the chain of command doesn't count. The fact that I had confronted Claudia was not considered whistleblowing. It was not enough. I needed to ventilate the cover-up more publicly and outside of the Justice Department.

Fortunately, DC's attorney ethics rules allow a government lawyer to reveal client confidences or secrets "when permitted or authorized by law." At least in theory, disclosures permitted by the Whistleblower Protection Act, even those that are not compelled, would not violate the ethics rules for government attorneys. The provision recognizes the "unique circumstances raised by attorney-client relationships within the government." There was also favorable precedent from the Clinton era, which held that a government agency could not invoke a privilege to prevent a government lawyer from providing evidence of the possible commission of criminal offenses within the government. In my circumstances, the Justice Department wanted to use the attorney-client privilege as both a sword and a shield, accusing me of breaching the privilege by revealing the government's misconduct, while hiding behind the privilege to commit illegal acts. But there is no privilege to break the law. Period. The attorney-client relationship cannot be used to further a crime.

I looked up the contact information for Michael Isikoff, *Newsweek's* veteran investigative reporter, whom I had heard on the radio that morning toeing the Justice Department's party line. He broke the Monica Lewinsky story, and much of what he uncovered led directly to the formal inquiry and ultimate impeachment of President Clinton. I certainly could not be accused of going to a flaming Democrat. I called him and told him he was wrong when he said that the Justice Department never thought that Lindh was represented by counsel—and I had the emails to prove it.

I went to Kinkos, an office and print center, and faxed the emails to him. I then went to see Mario, my stylist and surrogate therapist.

"Cut it all off," I said.

"Are you sure?" he asked.

"Yes," I said with a newfound certainty.

He tied my hair close to my scalp, braided it into a thick rope, cut it off, and placed it in a plastic bag. The other women in foils and curlers started clapping at my bold Sinead O'Connor look. I donated my hair to "Locks of Love," which makes wigs for kids with medical hair loss. Cutting my hair was a symbolic act, the physical manifestation of my blowing the whistle. It was liberating. I was free. That night was the first time I was able to sleep soundly in months.

That was how I became *Newsweek's* source. I hate the terms "leak" and "leaker" because what I really did was make a lawful disclosure as a whistleblower of my own emails, which would not have existed had I not resurrected them from the bowels of my computer's archives. But I won't get into the semantics because it is irrelevant to what followed.

Suffice it to say, I was unaware whether any of my emails had reached the court at the time I made the disclosure, and I had a more-than-reasonable belief that they had not. If one had reviewed the docket sheet at the time, it was like reading tea leaves because everything was under seal, meaning secret. One could discern only that at some point in April, the court granted one of the government's numerous sealed motions for a protective order concerning "thirty-three documents" submitted to the court *ex parte* (by only one side) for *in camera* (by only the judge) review. These "documents" were never identified as email, much less *my* emails. They could have been memos, faxes, telephone logs, or take-out menus for all I knew. As I've explained, Claudia deliberately concealed from me both the existence and substance of the court's orders and, what was done with the missing emails I recovered.

*Newsweek* published a searing exclusive on "The Lindh Case Emails," which featured the graphic picture of a naked Lindh, bound and blindfolded, with his hands covering his genitals. The hard copy of the article contained only two sentences from my emails, but at least now the information was in the public domain. I deliberately asked not to be quoted because I was trying to remain anonymous. This was not about fame or profit. A quote from me would be a big red arrow pointing to me as the source. However, my emails, including my name, were published in full on *Newsweek's* website. Whether *Newsweek* meant to or not, it had burned its source—me. Reporters willing to protect their sources became a litmus test when I started representing whistleblowers years later.

Soon I got a call from Joan "reminding" me of my professional obligations. It turns out, Claudia was on vacation in Europe when the story broke.

After the *Newsweek* article, the court requested that the Department of Justice file a pleading in three weeks "addressing whether any documents ordered protected by the court were disclosed by any person bound by an Order of this court." The Justice Department used this order as a pretext to launch an overreaching criminal investigation.

I was never bound by, or even aware of, any court order protecting documents (Claudia later admitted in a sworn affidavit that she was not sharing the court's orders with me) and I clearly fell outside the court's purview after I left the Department of Justice. Two years later, Judge Ellis unsealed a November 2002 order in which he held exactly that: "[I]t appears to the Court that [Ms. Radack's] disclosure does not technically constitute a violation of any Order of this Court." But it had not stopped the Department from relentlessly pursuing me for the next four years.

The Justice Department never bothered to share this exculpatory order with me, even after it was unsealed. Quite to the contrary, it used the opposite assertion (that I had violated the court's sealing order) as the justification for its retaliation. The Justice Department used the court's earlier order as a pretext to harass, intimidate, financially cripple, and ruin me professionally; get me fired from my law firm; launch a bad-faith, retaliatory criminal investigation that lasted for the next year and a half; make bar referrals, one of which is still pending today; and put me on the "No-Fly" list.

# THE LINDH CASE IMPLODES

I N LATE JUNE 2002, Agent Ron Powell of the Justice Department's Office of Inspector General phoned me at work to ask me questions about the *Newsweek* article. Like most unsuspecting whistleblowers, I was inclined to cooperate. Little did I know that Agent Powell was about to become the Inspector Javert of my life, pursuing me relentlessly and obsessively and making a normal life almost impossible.

Every major federal agency has an Office of Inspector General (IG). A primary purpose of the office is to investigate reports of internal fraud, waste, or abuse. The IG staff is usually divided between financial audits and investigations. While Congress established these offices to be independent, they often are not. In agencies like Justice, the Inspector General is nominated by the president and confirmed by the Senate. The IG reports to the head of the agency and serves at the pleasure of the president. In other words, if an IG is rocking the administration's boat too much, he or she can be instantly removed. The IG's performance appraisal comes from the agency head, who also controls the issuance of awards and financial bonuses to the IG. As a consequence, IGs are often quite political in their selection of cases for investigation and the manner in which the findings are cast.

However, Justice's longstanding IG, Glenn Fine, had a good reputation—at least when it came to going after the "baby agencies" that the Department of Justice oversaw: the FBI, INS, DEA, and Bureau of Prisons.

I had a quixotic view of the IG as a kind of knight in shining armor—an outside, objective force riding over the hill to save me from the wrath of the Justice Department. My trust in the IG was misplaced. The IG is a bureaucracy just like any other, with all the problems and limitations PRAO suffered. The IG controls the investigation. Often the IG initiates a probe in response to a scandal first raised in the media. And often, the only real investigation that emanates from the IG centers not on the problem, but on the person who raised the problem. It is not unusual for the employee who made the report of misconduct to find him or herself the subject of the real investigation—and that is what happened to me. I later witnessed a different IG completely double-cross a group of whistleblowers when I represented a former National Security Agency (NSA) official named Thomas Drake eight years later.

I cooperated initially with the IG and tried to steer Agent Powell towards the issue of why someone would leak the emails at issue, but he clearly had no intention of going there. All he cared about was plugging the leak. When he called me at work out of the blue, he tried to manipulate me into committing to dates and times I had already told him I couldn't remember; for example, he asked when I had eaten lunch with Don and another friend. I told him that it was sometime two weeks earlier, but I didn't remember the exact day. He then tried to deduce the date for me by calculating it based on amateur logic. "Well, you know it wasn't Friday, and Monday wouldn't make sense, so you had lunch on Wednesday, right?"

"No," I said. "I already told you, I don't remember the exact day and I'm not going to make guesses."

The same sort of questioning continued. His tone grew increasingly accusatorial and antagonistic, and I found myself feeling defensive, and my answers becoming increasingly Clinton-esque, responding to only the exact question that was asked in a very literal way. I felt he was trying to paint me into a corner and get me to commit to things about which I was unsure. I would tell him I didn't know something, and then he would repeat the same information according to his own narrative and ask me to agree.

"So you never called *Newsweek* or sent emails to *Newsweek* or faxed *Newsweek*? Records would never indicate that?" he demanded.

"I never said that. I could have returned a call to *Newsweek* or replied to an email. Do you want to search my computer and phone records?" I asked.

"If it comes to that, we will," he said ominously.

"Then I really have to go, Mr. Powell. I'll call you back."

Instead, I called a lawyer. I reached a friend of mine, Dan Jacobs, for advice. Years earlier, he had made disclosures of government wrong-doing, to which Assistant Attorney General Lois Schiffer issued an order prohibiting him from speaking to his own lawyers and made veiled threats of criminal prosecution if he did so. He challenged that order and won.

Jacobs recommended that I speak with Rick Robinson (probably best known for representing former National Security Advisor John Poindexter in the Iran-Contra scandal) of Fulbright & Jaworski. Meanwhile, the investigator left a number of similar messages, which luckily were memorialized on my voice mail. Jacobs also recommended that I create a contemporaneous record of my conversation with Agent Powell and transcribe one of Powell's messages. This was one of the best pieces of advice I ever received. When retaliation starts, whistleblowers should document everything.

One of Powell's messages stated: "I just want to emphasize this is a voluntary interview and a voluntary conversation, so if you don't want to talk to me anymore, that's fine, that's your prerogative."

Two weeks later, on July 12, 2002, the Defense Department was apoplectic that its new policy on torture of captives in the war on terrorism was going to be exposed. It was a Friday and Lindh's suppression hearing was scheduled to begin on Monday. The Defense Department made it clear to the Justice Department that it wanted the suppression hearing blocked. Michael Chertoff, the assistant attorney general for the Criminal Division who was overseeing all of Justice's terrorism prosecutions, had the prosecution team offer a deal: The serious charges against Lindh (e.g., terrorism, attempted murder, conspiracy to kill Americans, etc.) would be dropped and he would plead guilty to just two technical charges—providing aid to the Taliban and carrying a weapon.

The first charge, that by serving as a soldier in Afghanistan he had violated anti-Taliban economic sanctions, was merely a regulatory infraction. The second charge, that he had carried a rifle and two grenades while serving as a volunteer soldier in the national army of Afghanistan, failed to note that Lindh had never fired his gun and surrendered his weapons to General Dostum long before encountering any Americans. The government dropped all ten of its original terrorism charges.

Chertoff, at the Defense Department's insistence, demanded that Lindh sign a statement swearing he had "not been intentionally mistreated" by his US captors and waiving any future right to claim torture—a disclaimer that spoke for itself. Ultimately, the plea effectively prevented early exposure of the United States' torture policy.

Lindh, whose attorneys dreaded a trial near the Pentagon on the first anniversary of 9/11, in the most conservative judicial district in the country, accepted the deal and its stiff twenty-year sentence. Chertoff sealed the plea agreement with a "special administrative measure"—in effect, a gag order—barring Lindh from discussing his experience for the duration of his sentence. But that didn't stop his parents. As the ten-year anniversary of 9/11 approached, Frank Lindh wrote an op-ed for the *New York Times* in which he stated that his son "was subjected to physical and psychological abuse—a precursor to the mistreatment of many prisoners, in both Afghanistan and Iraq, by the American military during the George W. Bush era."

On the Monday morning that Lindh's suppression hearing was due to begin, in accordance with the deal negotiated over the weekend, Lindh pleaded guilty to the two relatively minor charges. The bombshell plea agreement, which startled even the judge, was announced before a packed courtroom awaiting the start of what was to be a crucial evidentiary hearing on whether statements Lindh made while in custody in Afghanistan—the ones I had advised the US against soliciting without counsel—could be used against him at his trial—which I had also advised against.

Ashcroft hailed the Justice Department's anemic performance as "an important victory in America's war on terrorism." I think if it was a victory for anyone, however, it was a victory for Lindh. As Ashcroft had ominously noted six months earlier, "Walker Lindh could receive multiple life sentences, six additional ten-year sentences, plus thirty years" in jail. The twenty-year sentence was half of what he faced if convicted on the two minor charges. He could be released in seventeen years. Lindh had won a future. It seemed like a good deal at the time.

As Jane Mayer of *The New Yorker* would later explain, "[I]n the Lindh case prosecutorial zeal appears to have weakened, rather than strengthened, the government's hand, contributing to a record of error that hastened the eventual settlement of the case on diminished charges."

Did I cause the government's case to collapse? No, the government sank its own case by cutting corners and overreaching. In the words spoken by Talleyrand two centuries ago, "Above all, not too much zeal."

Little did I realize that I had unleashed the full force of the entire executive branch.

In a fifty-page Justice Department memo dated August 1, 2002—dubbed the "torture memo" when it became public two years later—Bybee of the Justice Department advised White House Counsel Gonzales that torturing al Qaeda terrorists detained abroad "may be justified" and that international laws against torture "may be unconstitutional if applied to interrogations" conducted in the war on terrorism. It was not discussed or shared with the Joint Chiefs of Staff or the State Department. The Justice Department had learned its lesson about sharing controversial memos with likely dissenters.

The memo drew a sharp distinction between torture, "an egregious extreme act," and the more vague "cruel, inhuman or degrading" treatment of detainees. According to the Justice Department, inflicting moderate or fleeting pain does not constitute torture; instead, physical torture must cause pain so severe that it "rise[s] to . . . the level that would ordinarily be associated with . . . death, organ failure, or serious impairment of bodily functions"—lifting language from a Medicare statute (setting out the conditions under which hospitals must provide emergency medical care) wholly unrelated to torture. For a cruel or inhuman technique to rise to the level of *psychological* torture, the mental harm must last "months or even years," making it impossible to determine at the time it is inflicted.

Even under the Justice Department's extreme definition, the United States still committed torture at its detention facilities. That Justice

Department officials knew that their proposal was legally shaky comes across in the memo's suggestion that "necessity or self-defense could provide justifications that would eliminate any criminal liability." Never mind that if Rwanda or the former Yugoslavia made these arguments in front of a war crimes tribunal, they would be laughed right out of court.

After the memo leaked, President Bush, with his selective amnesia, said that he could not remember whether he had seen it—as if a memo on such a macabre issue would not make a lasting impression. The Justice Department responded to the leak by disavowing the memo, calling parts of it overbroad and irrelevant, and promising to rewrite and replace it with a new memo more carefully addressing the question of proper interrogation techniques for al Qaeda and Taliban detainees. But the White House and Justice Department's face-saving public relations effort was nothing more than a transparent attempt at damage control to contain the diplomatic and political backlash caused by US-sanctioned torture. The government's repudiation of the memo was not at all credible and the rejected version was not replaced by the intransigent administration for another six months.

The memo lay the groundwork for the government's overall thinking about interrogation of terror detainees. While it only addressed the treatment of al Qaeda detainees in CIA custody, it provided the legal underpinnings for subsequent abuse of prisoners in Afghanistan and Iraq, and the Defense Department relied on it in crafting a much longer and harsher secret Pentagon report in March 2003, which examined the logistical, policy, and legal issues surrounding the interrogation of detainees at Guantánamo Bay, Cuba.

Obviously, "exercising my prerogative" (in the words of Agent Powell) to decline speaking with him was *not* fine because on August 15, he called my new law firm and told the receptionist, the office manager, and a partner that he was conducting a "criminal investigation" of me and that the firm had "just hired a criminal." I had not received a subject or target letter, not been named a suspect (or even a "person of interest," Bush-speak for branding someone guilty when they didn't have enough evidence to bring a real case), never been arrested, and never been criminally charged, prosecuted, or convicted. When the investigator sought phone and fax records, one of the DC partners referred him to a managing partner in Hawkins's New York office, W. Cullen MacDonald. Suffice it to say, the investigator's inflammatory contact with over half the people in my small DC branch office excited much anxiety on the part of my law firm—and it certainly intimidated and rattled me.

Two weeks later, I got a letter from Justice's Office of Professional Responsibility (OPR), the internal disciplinary component, requesting information about a case I was involved in that was unrelated to the Lindh case. My attorney thought it might be a back-door way of talking to me about the Lindh matter or retaliation for my refusal to speak to the IG or for embarrassing PRAO. Working at the Department of Justice had gone from being a source of pride to a Kafkaesque nightmare from which I could not wake. It was not enough to have forced me out of my government job—they were trying to ruin my career. How much damage could one vengeful bureaucracy inflict on me? The Department's incessant harassment knew no bounds and these over-the-top calls to my private employer were only the beginning.

Agent Powell continued to hound anyone who had the misfortune of being associated with me. I learned from Don Mackay that Powell insisted on knowing when Don, Jim, and I had lunch. Powell asked leading questions with factually incorrect predicates: "Was it right after Jim said that Isikoff contacted him that Jesselyn said that she talked to Isikoff?"

"Jesselyn never said that at all," Don insisted, accurately. "You're putting words in my mouth."

Then Agent Powell went back and interviewed Jim. Jim later told Don, "He had me coming and going. He was trying to convince me that Jesselyn told us she spoke to Isikoff. I'm eighty-four and my memory is still intact, but he was really confusing me, talking me in circles."

I felt just awful that my friends were paying a price for associating with me. I didn't tell my secret to anyone, including my husband, for precisely that reason; I wanted to give them plausible deniability. I didn't want my colleagues, friends, or family dragged into this quagmire—or worse, to be in a position where they would have to implicate me. I wanted them to be able to say honestly that we had never discussed it.

The anniversary of 9/11 came and went. The Jewish new year followed shortly after, and again, I tried to draw strength from the liturgy, but now my focus was different: "O Source of mercy, give us the grace to show forbearance of those who offend against us. When the wrongs and injustices of others wound us, may our hearts not despair of human good. May no trial, however severe, embitter our souls and destroy our trust."

I wouldn't go so far as to say I was despairing, embittered, and destroyed. I was more hurt, uncertain, angry, and worried. The prayer continued:

> When beset by trouble and sorrow, our mothers and fathers put on the armor of faith and fortitude. May we too find strength to meet adversity with quiet courage and unshaken will. Help us to understand that injustice and hate will not forever afflict the human race; that righteousness and mercy will triumph in the end.

The words applied to my personal situation and to the ongoing war on terrorism more generally.

Luckily, at the annual firm dinner, I met Cullen MacDonald in person and he was very supportive and reassuring. "Everyone who works for the government gets investigated at one point or another," he joked. "It's almost a rite of passage inside the Beltway. It builds thick skin." My husband and I ended up in assigned seating across from him at dinner, whether by design or coincidence, and enjoyed hours of pleasant conversation with this affable and very paternal man.

After a month of the government leaning on him, however, MacDonald changed his tune. On October 1, he wrote a terse email to my attorney "at the instruction of our firm's Management Committee to apprise you of the circumstantial evidence presently under consideration by the Inspector General of the Department of Justice." He attached an outline of the "evidence," which basically documented Isikoff's calling and reaching my voice mail four times, and my speaking with him twice and sending him a fax.

Could the Justice Department have obtained an order for a pen register on Isikoff? Could it have secured an order for a tap-and-trace device on me? Post-Watergate regulations adopted by the Department of Justice establish a clear procedure for subpoenaing a journalist's phone records. First, the government must take all other reasonable steps to obtain the information sought before subpoenaing or approaching reporters in an investigation. Second, once the government has exhausted all other reasonable steps, the department can seek a subpoena of the reporter's phone records from a court, but must notify the reporter so that he or she may contest the request. Third, only under extraordinary circumstances and with the direct authorization of the attorney general can federal agents subpoena a reporter's records from the phone company without the reporter's knowledge, but the agents must inform the reporter within forty-five days that they have done so.

These guidelines were not followed in my case. Douglas McCollam wrote an article for the *Columbia Journalism Review* on my "creepy" situation appropriately titled "Who's Tracking Your Calls? And How Far Will the Department of Justice Go to Burn a Leaker?" He issued a prescient warning: "The government got a record of Isikoff's calls to an important source on an important story, without either party's knowing about it. It's a quick lesson on how far an irate government may go to burn your source. So remember, even on a local line, let's be careful out there." (None of us knew at that point that the government was already engaged in illegal warrantless wiretapping.)

I frantically called Isikoff. "I need a copy of the fax I sent you from Hawkins or else I'm going to be fired."

"I can't just hand it over to you," he said. "Have your attorney call me about it."

So I paid Rick $200 to pick up the phone and ask Isikoff to send it. Luckily, the "smoking fax," which was just my law review article, matched the time, date, and duration of the fax in the IG's flimsy arsenal of "evidence" with which the law firm confronted me. I had not sent secret government documents from the firm. It was just my boring scholarship.

Regardless of whether the Justice Department traced Isikoff's calls and shared the results with the law firm or traced the law firm's calls, the thing that was most disturbing was how Orwellian it all seemed. By 2011, in the words of reporter James Risen, whom the government unsuccessfully subpoenaed twice under Bush and once under Obama to testify against a whistleblower:

> ABC News reported on May 15, 2006, that senior federal law enforcement officials had informed them that the government was tracking the phone numbers of journalists

without the journalists' knowledge . . . [T]he government was tracking the incoming and outgoing numbers
called and received on the journalists' phones . . . I was
mentioned by name as one of the reporters whose work
the government was looking into . . . If the Government
was, in fact, tracking who I was speaking to on the phone,
then it can attempt to learn the identity of potential
confidential sources . . . I have [now] learned from an
individual who testified before a grand jury . . . that
the Government had shown this individual copies of
telephone records relating to calls made to and from me.

Risen hit back in a way that I wished Isikoff would have.

The telephone shenanigans were just one example of the Justice
Department blatantly violating its own internal regulations. The
Department of Justice shared details and evidence of an ongoing federal investigation with my private employer, impugned the reputation
of an uncharged third party (me), and was using my employer as an
instrument to accomplish what it otherwise could not. In the investigation of the anthrax "person of interest," Dr. Stephen Hatfill, which
was running concurrent to the investigation of me, the Department
similarly violated its own regulations, engaging in character assassination instead of criminal charge, defamation instead of due process,
and innuendo instead of evidence. It's what the government does
when it cannot make a case.

Hatfill's eventual lawsuit against the government described the
hypocrisy of the Department's tactics with regard to the two of us:

[The Justice Department's] half-hearted effort to identify
the source of these defamatory leaks [about Hatfill] stands
in stark contrast to the enormous resources brought to

bear in other cases in which information that the DOJ considers embarrassing has been leaked to the press. The disparate treatment makes one thing clear: Leaks that embarrass the DOJ are treated seriously and lead to criminal referrals (as in the case of DOJ employee Jesselyn Radack), while leaks that DOJ and FBI view as helpful (by placing organizations in a good light) are ignored.

This hypocrisy became even more blatant when Obama began prosecuting "unauthorized leaks" (compared to the administration's own "authorized leaks," an oxymoron) by public servants who were more often than not whistleblowers trying to correct wrongdoing.

Six years after his lawsuit, the government paid Hatfill a settlement valued at nearly $6 million that all but exonerated him. A month later, Bruce Ivins, the real culprit, committed suicide. Hatfill's case epitomized how impressive-looking condemnations can be built entirely on sand—a lesson learned the hard way in my own case and that equipped me to combat this phenomenon eight years later in representing former NSA official Thomas Drake in Obama's bellwether leak prosecution.

MacDonald emailed me that the management committee was inclined to ask for my resignation. The Justice Department was leaning heavily on them, and Hawkins was clearly playing hardball with me. MacDonald was unapologetic about the firm's willingness to act as an agent of the government. It seemed like the most exciting thing that had happened to him in decades. My immediate supervisors told me that many people on the management committee thought that MacDonald's tone in the email was too harsh.

A few days later I was still dodging bullets when I ran into MacDonald skulking around our small DC branch (he normally worked in the New York headquarters.) He looked very sheepish, as if I had caught him with his hand in the cookie jar—nosing around my office, to be more precise.

"You should know that at this very moment, Agent Powell is interviewing your boss and may be walking around here," he said, seeming very flustered. Then his tone grew more ominous. "The investigator is near the end of his investigation and is ready to *take action.*"

As visions flashed through my head of the police breaking down my door and forcing me to do the perp walk in front of the neighborhood soccer moms, I started to panic. To say that I was scared doesn't capture the depth of my fear.

That night, we went to "family swim" at the neighborhood pool to try to take my mind off the possibility of being arrested. My husband tried to reassure me.

"You're pregnant! That's why you're so emotional. I just know it. And look at how buoyant you are!"

I woke up the next morning with my nightgown soaked in blood and burst into tears.

My lawyer informed Hawkins in no uncertain terms that I was a federal whistleblower, and proved—by producing the fax cover sheet with the date, time, and length of transmission—that the damning fax the IG claimed was my "leaking secret government documents" from my law firm was nothing more than my sending Isikoff a copy of the law review article I had written. He assured the management committee that I neither used the firm's facilities to provide government materials to a member of the press, nor engaged in any other act that violates the ethical obligations of the bar; in fact, I provided information to the IG while simply protecting my own legal and constitutional rights to be free from further harassment and retaliation by the government.

On the same day, my attorney also sent a letter to the IG spelling out my allegations in no uncertain terms:

> While Ms. Radack worked at PRAO, she took several steps to thwart efforts by others within that office to conceal material regarding the Lindh case from the court. As a result of those actions she was subjected to a series of unlawful, retaliatory acts, all in violation of [the Whistleblower Protection Act]. We believe that the actions of Special Agent Powell are intended to further that retaliation against Ms. Radack by interfering with her current employment and otherwise besmirching her reputation.

On October 11, 2002, officers at the Guantánamo prison camp asked their superiors for permission to use harsher interrogation methods against inmates. Major General Michael Dunlavey, the commanding general at Guantánamo, asked his commander to approve the use of threats to convince the detainee that death or severely painful consequences are imminent for him and/or his family, a wet towel and dripping water to induce the perception of drowning, stress positions, exposure to cold temperatures or water, and menacing dogs. Dunlavely's legal advisor had reviewed these techniques and deemed them legal under the Geneva Conventions "so long as there is an important governmental objective" and the tactics are not used "for the purpose of causing harm or with the intent to cause prolonged" mental or physical suffering. (When suffocation by water was used by the Pinochet dictatorship in Chile, the State Department didn't hesitate to call it torture.)

That same day, the government filed an *ex parte* sealed document in the Lindh matter that "relates solely to the unauthorized disclosure of certain documents filed in this case by persons other than the defendant or member of the defense team." That must have been the major "action" to which Cullen MacDonald was cryptically referring. It was the "leak report." It all should have ended right there. Just like it should have ended after Lindh pleaded guilty.

On October 25, 2002, Dunlavey's commander expressed unease with the legal advisor's assessment of the new interrogation techniques and asked the chairman of the Joint Chiefs of Staff, General Richard Myers, for guidance: "I am uncertain whether all the techniques . . . are legal under US law, given the absence of judicial interpretation of the US statute. I am particularly troubled by the use of implied or express threats of death of the detainee and his family."

# SNIPERS

Two weeks later, the management committee gave me an affidavit stating that I had not leaked my email to *Newsweek* and told me in Johnnie Chochran-esque terms to "sign or resign." Once again I found myself in the middle of the night wide awake with worry about what to do. I wanted to cry, but was too angry. If anyone had told me a year earlier that the government would force me out, be lying to my private employer, and be trying to destroy me personally and professionally, I never would have believed it.

But now I was a caged bird—afraid to go to the grocery store for fear of running into former PRAO co-workers who lived nearby, afraid to leave my office for fear of running into anyone from the Department of Justice (it was only a block away), afraid to go to work (because I might be fired that day), afraid to go to sleep (because I'd have nightmares), and afraid to wake up (because I'd realize the nightmares were real). Most of all, I was afraid of the years this would rob from my life.

Rick Robinson recommended that I consult an employment lawyer, so I retained one of DC's top guns, Mona Lyons. She's a tough-as-nails attorney with a heart of gold, a great sense of humor, and a brilliant mind. I sent her firm all of Rick's correspondence to give them a flavor of what was going on. She asked if we could meet in person. When I got there, Mona and her colleagues spoke with me for nearly two hours. I will never forget it. It was the first time I felt not only supported in what I had done, but also *wronged* by what had followed. The experience with them legitimized my feelings of being unceremoniously forced out first by the Justice Department and now by my law firm. My case presented a number of novel legal issues. There was the post-employment retaliation by the Justice Department via my new employer. There was the public policy exception to the usual employment at-will doctrine, an exception I fit into as a whistleblower—a fact about which Rick had done an excellent job of putting the firm on notice. Therefore, to fire me for that reason (being a whistleblower) is unlawful because public policy favors blowing the whistle and it was not my performance with which Hawkins had a problem.

We decided to try to put the pin back in the grenade. Because of the IG's ongoing investigation of the underlying issues, its duty to investigate my whistleblower claims, and that my conduct was protected by law and public policy, I did not sign the affidavit. Plus, it was clear that the management committee at Hawkins wanted me to execute the affidavit for ulterior reasons, namely for the benefit of the government, which exhibited no interest whatsoever in investigating the underlying cover-up that had actually occurred.

By sick coincidence, a serial sniper was terrorizing the DC region. Eleven people had been shot in the sniper attacks since October, and nine had died. The most recent shooting occurred at the hardware store that was practically our second home. The kids' outdoor recess and gym classes were canceled.

So, in a parallel universe, some killer was literally hunting people in our neighborhood. And on a personal level, I felt stalked by the Justice Department, which was going after me with both barrels and an endless supply of artillery and ammunition. I felt as if the rapacious agency would go to the ends of the earth to destroy me. There was no visible end in sight. It was as if they were trying to stop me from practicing law, trying to intimidate me, and trying to break me—and they were succeeding.

I was running on fumes, holding it together with gum and a shoestring. The serial sniper shot two more people. But the generalized anxiety I (and the rest of the DC metropolitan area) felt over the serial sniper was paralleled by an acute anxiety I felt waiting to hear from the management committee. Waiting for the other shoe to drop was giving me *agita*—that existential dyspepsia of the soul. It had a huge effect on my psyche, my health, my very core. As an adult, the feeling of dread was no different from when I was five. It took me back to my childhood, learning that my parents were separated but not yet divorced—something I mistakenly believed was my fault and that I had the power to stop.

On October 24, 2002, police caught the sniper who had paralyzed the region that month. There were actually two—the malevolent adult and an unquestioning adolescent follower blinded by a father-figure who promised to protect him.

"Aren't you relieved?" a friend and Hawkins colleague, Jill Chessen, emailed me.

Yes, I was relieved momentarily, until I received an email from Cullen MacDonald telling me that the management committee was placing me on a leave of absence starting the following day. The heavy-handed tactic of placing me on leave and giving me one day's notice again took me by surprise. My hands grew ice cold, I started shaking, and I became short of breath. Oddly enough, I still felt determined to finish my work. For having professed doubts about my trustworthiness, the firm continued to give me substantive assignments and attorney-client matters to handle until the moment I left. I even worked late on my last day.

On November 4, 2002, Major General Miller took command of the Guantánamo prison camp with a mandate to get more and better information from the prisoners. He ran a much tighter ship and placed a premium on clarifying the responsibilities of his subordinates. Two days later, Patrick Philbin, a deputy in the Justice Department's Office of Legal Counsel, laid out in a secret, lengthy memo to the White House the legal basis for the administration's approach to military tribunals. The memo said that the president has "inherent authority," as commander in chief, to establish military tribunals without Congressional authorization, and that the attacks of 9/11 were "plainly sufficient" to warrant applying the laws of war. It suggested that the White House could apply international law selectively and that trying terrorists under the laws of war "does not mean that terrorists will receive the protections of the Geneva Conventions." The memo opened a debate that would later divide the Bush administration and continue well into the Obama administration. Efforts to prosecute alleged terrorists before military commissions were struck down by the Supreme Court during the Bush years, but the Obama administration persisted in trying to revive them.

My attorney and I met with MacDonald a week later, which turned out to be a wasted trip to New York and an exercise in futility and frustration. MacDonald had morphed from a kindly old man to a Sherlock Holmes wannabe—condescending, rude, and completely ignorant of employment law generally and whistleblower law in particular. He kept saying that he wanted to explore "option enlarging" strategies, but what he really wanted to know were the salacious details of what happened in the Lindh affair. This approach put me in an impossible situation because it would have entailed violating the very attorney-client privilege I was being accused by the Justice Department of breaching. He told me unambiguously, "All the DC partners love your work." But he also said that even if I made a valid disclosure under the Whistleblower Protection Act, he disagreed with my "judgment." Again, I was damned if I did and damned if I didn't give him what he wanted.

Moreover, Hawkins was really tying my hands. I was not getting paid but I couldn't apply for unemployment benefits because I was technically still employed there. They were trying to force my resignation. I refused to give in.

"Mommy, are you going to die?" my two-year-old asked me one evening.

"Goodness no, Sam! Why would you ask such an awful thing?" I ventured, fearing that in his toddler mind he somehow grasped that I had multiple sclerosis.

"Because I heard you tell Anna's mom that you were going to be fired."

Sam was equating being "fired" with being "shot," a term that was all over the news because of the snipers. It demonstrated the very literal way that toddlers often interpret the world. But it broke my heart that the work situation had trickled down to my kids in this kind of way.

Hawkins paid me for one month. Without the courtesy of providing any notice, they cut off my pay the next month, even though their attorney, Betsy Plevan, insisted to Mona that no such decision had been reached. Plevan asked if I would agree to a suspension without pay on a Tuesday, but the letter cutting off my pay was postmarked Monday. As an equal breadwinner for my family, this was a double-whammy. I was no longer bringing in income, while at the same time I was racking up legal bills.

In a Pentagon memo dated November 27, 2002, the Defense Department's chief lawyer, Haynes, recommended that Rumsfeld approve the use of fourteen interrogation techniques on detainees at Guantánamo Bay, such as yelling at prisoners during questioning and using "stress positions," such as being forced to stand for up to four hours. Haynes also recommended approval of one technique among the harsher methods requested by US military authorities at Guantánamo: the use of "mild, non-injurious physical contact such as grabbing, poking in the chest with the finger and light pushing." However, he cautioned moderation, noting that while certain techniques were available as a matter of policy, blanket approval was not warranted at the time.

When Rumsfeld read Haynes's memo, he added a sarcastic hand-written note at the bottom: "I stand for eight to ten hours a day. Why is standing limited to four hours?" Rumsfeld issued an order allowing harsh interrogation techniques at Guantánamo. They included interrogating prisoners for twenty hours at a time, stripping them, threatening them with dogs, hooding them during interrogation, and forcibly shaving their heads and beards. Vice President Cheney would later tell CNN that the detainees were well-treated, well-fed, and "living in the tropics."

The unemployment rate that December was the highest it had been in nine years, and I was now effectively part of it. Rick drafted a letter to the IG, whom we hadn't heard from in over two months, asking Glenn Fine to inform us of what steps his office intended to take with respect to the whistleblower matters we raised. Rick's letter also noted that we learned that the IG had filed its secret leak report: "This filing, coupled with the lack of any response to Ms. Radack's allegations, would seem to suggest that the investigation regarding the Lindh matter has concluded."

Meanwhile, MacDonald sent Rick an email: "Last week you left word on my voice mail that you were trying to learn the status of the IG's investigation to see if the filing of its report with the court allowed you to have your client become more cooperative and forthcoming with the management committee. The ball is in her court."

Rick pointed out that he had written the IG twice and suspected that the IG would be much more forthcoming in responding to an inquiry from MacDonald because MacDonald was the one helping the IG with the investigation. It was ridiculous that MacDonald was trying to put the onus on *me* to determine the status of the government's investigation when *Hawkins* was the one in bed with the Justice Department.

Still, MacDonald continued to insist that *I* should be doing more in the way of bringing "this" to a close. Plevan asked what Rick thought the committee should do. He said that Hawkins should let me come back to work because I had provided them with an explanation of my contacts with Isikoff from the office, proved that they did not involve government information, and demonstrated that I was correct on the law.

MacDonald said that the management committee was still not convinced that the ethics rules allowed a non-compulsory disclosure of government wrongdoing. Rick said we disagreed, had addressed this point *ad nauseam* in our last letter, and the DC ethics rules on this were clear. MacDonald replied that the firm was still entitled to know how I "exercised my judgment" even if there was no ethical violation. The law firm appeared to be projecting *its* ethical shortcomings onto me. Rick suspected that the management committee was not going along with MacDonald's recommendations and may have wished to be more accommodating.

By the end of December, the firm was still in the same position it had been in at the beginning of the month, when their lawyer had promised a decision *that week*. The parties' stances had not changed. Hawkins needed to return me to work, put me back on paid leave, or fire me. If not, after a certain date, I could construe their actions as a constructive discharge and seek unemployment benefits.

The firm kept moving the target. Whenever I answered their questions, provided legal authority, or attended their kangaroo meetings, they came up with different requirements.

Rick received another missive from MacDonald. It was the second time MacDonald stated my "disclosure of privileged communications to the news media" as if it were a foregone conclusion. Like the IG, the management committee was trying to put words in my mouth—the reason I terminated my initial cooperation with the IG. To be clear, I had told the management committee only that I engaged in conduct protected by the Whistleblower Protection Act. I didn't tell them what that conduct entailed. As some sort of grand favor, MacDonald said that Hawkins was "allowing" me to stay on unpaid leave for two more months. It was like Claudia saying that she would hold the vitriolic performance evaluation in abeyance until I found another job.

Three women whistleblowers in high-profile cases were named as "Persons of the Year" for 2002 by *TIME Magazine*. I don't agree with the gendered construction of whistleblowing that the media painted. I am not a biological essentialist who embraces the valorization of difference. In my case, the bad actors included just as many women as men, and women had certainly not cornered the market on integrity. But the *TIME* article still uplifted me. Sherron Watkins, Cynthia Cooper, and Coleen Rowley's advice was to stand up and do the right thing. It provided a glimmer of light after a low point on the roller coaster created by the law firm's latest salvo.

MacDonald called Rick on December 30, 2002, pressuring him to call the IG and telling Rick how to do his job. It was almost as if

MacDonald was scared of the IG. Maybe it wasn't so fun being the IG's tool after all.

Dan and I met with Mona Lyons on New Year's Eve. She agreed that I shouldn't resign, but she also thought that I should start looking for another job. Under DC law, I had been constructively discharged and was now eligible for unemployment compensation. It would have been difficult to sue Hawkins because I'd have to give them in discovery the information that I had been refusing to provide.

Dan, Rick, and I met with Tom Devine and Doug Hartnett of the Government Accountability Project—a nonprofit whistleblower organization—the next day. They were helpful and cleverly suggested that I tell MacDonald that if *he* got a waiver from the Justice Department (which would never happen), then I'd tell him anything and everything he wanted to know about the Lindh case. They also noted that the Justice Department was ignoring the *notice* I had put them on that the agency had been cutting corners in the Lindh case. The upshot of the meeting was that I needed to shift the spotlight off of myself and shine it onto Justice's conduct. I was dealing with an administration that was masterful at distractions, distortions, and changing the subject.

I updated my resume and started looking for another job. I went to the DC Department of Unemployment Services and applied for unemployment benefits, a humiliating experience at the time, but one with which many Americans would become quite familiar when a full-blown recession hit five years later. I became a card-carrying member of the ACLU. I emailed my law school mentors. I took the first baby steps in rebuilding my life and moving forward.

But it was only hours before the Justice Department stuck its leg in my path to trip me again.

At the end of the day on January 7, 2003, I returned a call from Rick. He said that Glenn Fine, the Inspector General himself, had called him with two pieces of bad news. First, the IG "looked into it" (my whistleblower allegations), and they "were not going to pursue it." My immediate reaction was that Fine didn't look very deeply. He didn't even bother to ask *me*, the whistleblower, what had happened. He didn't bother to interview the complainant!

The second piece of bad news, to add insult to injury, was that there was an open criminal investigation of *me* (for what, the IG would not specify) and that the IG decided to refer it to Stuart Nash in the DC US Attorney's Office for prosecution. I had friends in that office. It was all so surreal.

Rick assured me that the criminal matter was a dog case and not to lose sleep over it, but how could I not? I started a new law review article during my restless nights and finished it in less than a week. Lending credence to the adage that the personal is political, the article argued that blowing the whistle is an exception to the ethics rule governing confidentiality, especially in light of the fact that the rule was amended in 2002 to add a new exception to confidentiality in order "to comply with other law." The Whistleblower Protection Act, I argued, is precisely the kind of "other law" that should be recognized. I submitted it to *The Georgetown Journal of Legal Ethics*, which I learned was doing a symposium issue on whistleblowers. I did not want my article placed anywhere else, so I put all of my eggs in one basket and luckily my article was accepted.

In a January 15 memo, Rumsfeld asked Haynes to convene a working group to consider legal, policy, and operational issues relating to interrogation of detainees held by the US military in the war on terrorism. His decision was prompted at least in part by objections raised by some military lawyers who felt that the techniques approved for use at Guantánamo Bay might go too far. That same day, in another memo to the head of the US Southern Command, Rumsfeld rescinded his December 2 approval of some interrogation techniques for Guantánamo Bay. The new memo allowed commanders to seek Rumsfeld's direct approval to use the tougher methods if they were "warranted in an individual case" and referenced the other memo to Haynes.

That same day, Hawkins's attorney called Rick. It was a very odd conversation, as if Plevan had taken English lessons from Bush on how to speak in double negatives. Hawkins didn't want me *not* to work there. They went back and forth on the same old issues—Hawkins's "right" to know all of the details about Lindh and my inability to tell them. Rick told Hawkins's attorney that I wanted back pay and pay for the rest of the year if they wanted a release from a lawsuit. I was surprised Hawkins still wanted me to work there at all. It was probably more that the firm didn't want to get sued.

Rick called Stuart Nash at the US Attorney's Office for DC. Nash wasn't doing much with the case. "It's not on the back burner, but it's not on the front burner, either," he said.

Nash said he wasn't ready to talk about possible charges, but that he would let Rick know if he decided to go forward *and* if he decided not to, which was generous of him. He didn't have to do that. I think he saw the case for the witch hunt that it was. In the biggest surprise, the IG had *not* given Nash our letters claiming whistleblower protection. I hate to sound like a conspiracy theorist, but it seemed at best a sloppy oversight and, at worst, another cover-up. The fact that I was a whistleblower was information that could be exculpatory to any charge that Nash might bring. So much for the criminal justice system where investigations must have a clear objective and the information collected—and the means by which it is acquired—must ultimately be shared with the accused and tested in open court.

Rick said maybe it was time to go to the press. Mona agreed.

# AMAZING JANE

ON JANUARY 17, 2003, the Pentagon's Haynes designated the general counsel of the Air Force to head the working group that Rumsfeld requested in one of his January 15 memos. President Bush may not have known the particulars of American-led torture, but his public statements continued to suggest he had a pretty good idea. "All told, more than 3000 suspected terrorists have been arrested in many countries," he boasted in his State of the Union address in January 2003. "Many others have met a different fate. Let's put it this way—they are no longer a problem . . ."

On February 4, Jane Mayer of *The New Yorker* literally showed up on my doorstep. I was at the grocery store, but she left a message neatly penned on notebook paper.

> *Dear Jesselyn—*
> *I am really sorry to bother you like this, but I couldn't get a phone number to call. I'm writing for The New Yorker magazine, currently looking back at the Lindh-Walker case, and I hoped to interview you about it either*

*on or off the record. It seems your concerns were prescient,*
*so I was interested in your perspective . . .*

*Again, sorry for the imposition, but it's a serious*
*subject and I wanted to reach you.*

*All the best,*
*Jane Mayer*

As if I didn't know who she was! As if *The New Yorker* wasn't the only magazine to which I subscribed! I had been aching for a god-send like this. It was heartening to know that someone, especially an investigative journalist of Jane Mayer's caliber, was giving the John Walker Lindh matter a much-needed closer look.

My attorneys and I had been discussing going public, and Jane Mayer presented the perfect opportunity. It was a gift. Jane herself became one of the saving graces of my case and, more broadly, a national treasure in exposing the government's going to the "dark side"—torture—during the years following 9/11. She had been researching the article for months and focusing on government over-reaching in the Lindh case. Her note felt like divine intervention.

MacDonald, after continually ignoring our request that he respond to my severance proposal, called back Rick immediately when he got wind of the forthcoming article. Hawkins's attorney hit the roof. Plevan was furious and said I couldn't talk about anything having to do with Hawkins—namely, their treatment of me. Rick assured her that I would not discuss client matters, but that I had every right to discuss Hawkins's ugly conduct. Hawkins was nervous because they were easily recognizable to *The New Yorker* readers as the firm of famous novelist Louis Auchincloss.

Hawkins's attorney called Mona, saying that Hawkins "thought it was time for the employment lawyers to talk." Mona reiterated our position that they needed to respond to our severance proposal and that they couldn't stop me from talking to the press about the terms and conditions of my employment. The best indicator of malfeasance is fear of the truth.

During this time, a draft version of the Patriot Act II (again titled in patriotic-sounding words, the "Domestic Security Enhancement Act of 2003") leaked from the Justice Department. The Patriot Act II took the Patriot Act's civil liberties infringements even further. It provided for the power to wiretap Americans for fifteen days without a court order after terrorist attacks (it was still unknown at this point that the NSA was already conducting unfettered warrantless wiretaps on Americans), the ability to make secret arrests, and the power to strip American citizenship from anyone who helped an organization that the attorney general deemed to be a "terrorist." Chuck Lewis of the Center for Public Integrity, to which the legislation was disclosed, praised the "leaker" as a patriot and a hero who would be ruined professionally. I knew how correct he was.

Hawkins's lawyer left a voice mail message for Rick to see if they could move things forward. Basically, Plevan said the firm would propose two months' severance conditioned on a "non-disparagement" agreement. She said she didn't think the firm had a lot of flexibility, which was obviously bluster, but would try to get them to do a little better if Rick could get me closer to two months' severance.

In mid-February, I was awarded unemployment compensation benefits. It wasn't much, but enough to buy groceries and gas for the week.

Hawkins's lawyer called Rick to say that they didn't believe I could "control any journalist," a truism. Rick, with Mona's help, sent a blunt email saying that I had control over whether the firm would be identified in *The New Yorker* and that I obviously had complete control over whether I spoke to any other news outlets.

Rick also got a voice mail from Nash at the US Attorney's Office, which said that Nash expected to be in a position to tell Rick what he planned to do with the case in the next two to three weeks, but that he couldn't provide additional details. (It was interesting to see how the media got things moving.)

Cullen MacDonald sent Rick a threatening and desperate email:

> Because the firm would consider any mention of its name in a nationwide publication concerning your client . . . to be harmful to its reputation, it hereby requests that she exercise the power . . . she has to keep our name out of it. It is indisputable that any employee willfully causing disparaging publicity would be subject to immediate discharge.

MacDonald obviously needed to go back to law school. Any first-year student knows that speech is only defamatory if it's not true. If he thought the truth might "disparage" the firm, then that fact spoke for itself.

Besides, Hawkins, Delafield & Wood had already constructively discharged me. Additionally, I had no need or desire to disparage Hawkins. I would simply tell the truth. Private entities need to be held accountable, especially in this era of the rising national security state, with people like Cullen MacDonald more than happy to act as informants for our burgeoning Stasi. The Justice Department made him feel important and imbued him with a sense of adventure.

Rick strategized with Mona and wrote back:

> First, I had thought I had made clear that Ms. Radack was willing to exercise her ability to keep the firm's name out of the upcoming *New Yorker* article only as part of an

87

overall severance agreement. Second, we do not believe that the firm is treating Ms. Radack as an employee or that a recitation of the facts regarding the firm's treatment of an employee can provide cause for termination of the employee . . .

I loved my lawyers.

A week later, I received a "Notice of In-Person Hearing." Hawkins's lawyer had appealed the determination that granted me unemployment compensation—a determination that specifically found that I was "not discharged for misconduct." It was unclear how much the government was pulling Hawkins's strings, but Hawkins was certainly acting as vindictively as the government. I had been told Hawkins "wanted to stay on the government's good side," but this was beyond the pale.

As the office of unemployment compensation identified the issues, Hawkins claimed that I "voluntarily left last work without good cause . . ." and/or "was discharged for misconduct." Hawkins's attorney was sheepish about the whole thing when confronted and was making noises about the appeal having to be filed hastily in the wake of my "threats" to expose the firm to bad publicity. Mona told Plevan that appealing could turn out to be an expensive decision for Hawkins because, for a lousy couple of hundred dollars a week, they now had another stubborn lawyer to deal with. Mona also mentioned that the appeal really undermined Hawkins's *bona fides* about the underlying "ethics reason" (not being able to trust my judgment) for their decision-making.

Three days later I got the advance copy of *The New Yorker* article. In a sprawling investigative spread, Jane, who was privy to information I did not have, was able to document the cover-up:

An official list compiled by the prosecution confirms that the Justice Department did not hand over Radack's most critical email, in which she questioned the viability of Lindh's confession, until after her confrontation with Flynn.

Vindication at last! And from a well-respected magazine famed for its fact-checking department.

The next day I was bombarded with press inquiries from NPR, CBS News, "60 Minutes," and the *New York Times*. Conspicuously absent was the *Washington Post*, my local paper. I also received calls from former *New York Times* columnist Anthony Lewis, Legal Director of the ACLU Steve Shapiro, Senior Minority Counsel on the House Judiciary Committee Burt Wides, and the office of Congressman Waxman, who was the Ranking Democratic Member on the House Committee on Government Reform. Rick advised me to lay low and gauge the public reaction. It could either make the case against me harder to prosecute or make the Justice Department more determined to get me. If you hit the Justice Department too hard in public, they are locked in and need to discredit you.

Somewhere far away, white supremacists assaulted John Walker Lindh in prison.

Meanwhile, the Defense Department's chief counsel, Haynes, at the behest of Guantánamo Bay commanders, prepared a draft of a classified Pentagon report, dated March 6, 2003. The 100-plus page report's central argument was radical: Normal strictures on torture did not apply because nothing was more important than "obtaining intelligence vital to the protection of untold thousands of American citizens."

Much of the reasoning in the Pentagon report adopted the arguments of the January and August 2002 memos. The report outlined

US laws and international treaties forbidding torture and, using the Strangelovian logic of dictatorships and totalitarian regimes around the world, argued that those restrictions could be overcome by "national security" considerations or legal technicalities. In lock-step with the original Gonzales memo, the report advised that the president wasn't bound by domestic and international laws prohibiting torture because he has the authority as Commander-in-Chief to approve almost any physical or psychological actions during interrogation, up to and including torture. We had really gone off the rails.

Suspected terrorists could be treated like the alleged heretics hauled before the Inquisition. They were not allowed to mount a defense, innocence was wholly irrelevant, and creative torture was the preferred method for obtaining confessions.

This perversion of the Commander-in-Chief clause regressed the Constitution 800 years to a time before the Magna Carta. It flew in the face of years of Supreme Court precedent that had repeatedly rejected expansive claims of absolute control by the executive. In a famous legal case, *Youngstown Sheet and Tube Co. v. Sawyer* (conspicuously absent from the torture memos), the Supreme Court rejected President Truman's unilateral attempt to take over private steel mills to forestall a strike during the Korean War. Supreme Court Justice O'Connor, tellingly, would later cite this case in support of her statement that "a state of war is not a blank check for the president when it comes to the rights of the nation's citizens." While the president has significant latitude in the conduct of foreign affairs, this leeway has been constrained by congressional legislation and judicial decisions to prevent the transmogrification of the president into an absolute monarch. According to the increasingly espoused "unitary executive theory," President Bush could authorize abuse and still plausibly *claim*, as he had assured the public in the aftermath of the leaked Justice Department torture memo and Pentagon report, that he "adhere[s] to law." He testily told reporters, "That ought to comfort you." But Bush's reassurances were not comforting because his administration's documents argued that no law banning torture or regulating interrogation could bind the president when he is acting as Commander-in-Chief.

As Harold Koh, then dean of Yale Law School, pointed out, if the president has Commander-in-Chief power to commit torture, he has the power to order genocide, sanction slavery, institute apartheid, license summary execution, and commit numerous other human rights atrocities. Once Koh became the State Department's top legal advisor under Obama, however, Koh quickly embraced unilateral presidential intervention in Libya without Congressional approval.

The Pentagon report also advised that government agents and civilian or military personnel who might torture prisoners at the president's direction couldn't be prosecuted by the Justice Department for torture or other war crimes. With astonishing premeditation, it even outlined potential legal defenses, including the "necessity" of using torture to extract information to prevent an attack and the so-called "Nuremberg defense" of following "superior orders" that render moral choice illusory. The Nuremberg defense excuses questionable practices with the legal excuse that if actions were undertaken by command, then the burden of guilt is lifted. This was the legal argument used by the Nazi war criminals on trial after World War II. The judges at Nuremberg rejected this "just following orders" defense. The Yugoslav and Rwandan war crimes tribunals, which have been enforcing international criminal law more recently, have also rejected it.

But the Bush administration single-handedly and unilaterally redefined and reinstated torture. It officially endorsed principles relied on in the past by the military *juntas* in Argentina and Chile and by autocracies such as Algeria and Uzbekistan today, which claim that torture is justified when used to combat terrorism. Even if the administration's theories were never put into practice, as its officials stubbornly and repeatedly maintained, the report's revelation put a permanent stain on Jeffersonian democracy.

When the torture memo and the Pentagon report eventually became public in June 2004, the Bush administration refused to disclose, or even provide to Congress, copies of them, despite a fusillade of public condemnation stemming from leaks to several newspapers—and an independent press that was willing to print them. These memos revealed that the US government, acting carefully and with guidance from legal counsel, deliberately sought to skirt US and international laws.

At home, I watched *The Pentagon Papers* on TV. I had been an infant when Defense Department whistleblower Daniel Ellsberg leaked to the press the government's secret history of the Vietnam War. The White House and Justice Department tried to "neutralize" him. "It took months. It took over my life," his character said. Bush and Ashcroft were the second coming of Nixon and Mitchell. It sounded all too familiar. I later met Ellsberg, who is now a dear friend and partner in truth.

Bush was a more dishonest president than Richard Nixon, a conclusion supported by everyone from the predictable, such as former Vice President Al Gore, to Nixon's White House counsel, John Dean. The post-Watergate reforms, which were supposed to have reined in the government in response to earlier abuses and that were intended to prevent political harassment, were cast aside cavalierly. Never could I have imagined that the Obama administration, later elected on a reform platform of transparency, would prosecute more "leakers" (who more often than not were whistleblowers) than all previous presidential administrations combined.

Unbeknownst to me, on March 11, 2003, Senator Edward Kennedy submitted written questions to Ashcroft following a Judiciary

Committee hearing in early March on "The War Against Terrorism: Working Together to Protect America." Question nine was a page-long series of inquiries regarding my situation as reported in *The New Yorker*:

> Was Ms. Radack, in fact, forced to leave her position at the Justice Department because of the ethical advice she provided on the interrogation of Mr. Lindh? Have you conducted any investigation into the withholding of emails from the federal court in the Lindh case? Have any employees other than Ms. Radack been disciplined? Is Ms. Radack, in fact, now the target of a criminal investigation by the US Attorney's office? For what is she being investigated?

Senator Kennedy asked all the right questions. The Justice Department never responded.

From my experience, it was unlike the Justice Department to blow off inquiries from Congress, especially from someone of Kennedy's stature—the second most senior member of the Senate and one who served on the Judiciary Committee. I drafted a couple of congressional responses myself while at Justice and they were always given careful attention and review. But Ashcroft had a reputation for treating Congress as irrelevant.

The unemployment compensation hearing initiated by Hawkins was held on St. Patrick's Day. Everyone was clad in green, making for a comical sight that was quite fitting for the occasion. On the morning of the hearing, Agent Powell of the Justice Department met with Cullen MacDonald and Betsy Plevan at Hawkins to provide an affidavit to be presented to the Unemployment Compensation Appeals Division—something that Americans of any political stripe should find outrageous. Since when does the government orchestrate the firing of a private employee from the private sector and then encourage and assist the private employer in its effort to terminate the employee's receipt of unemployment benefits? The Justice Department's enlistment of a private law firm to act as its agent in retaliating against a former employee should offend the sensibilities of not just libertarians, but the most liberal Democrats and the most conservative Republicans.

The hearing lasted over three hours and was all over the map. Mona represented me brilliantly and was able to get MacDonald to admit that my "misconduct" was nothing more than the exercise of my constitutional right not to cooperate with a government investigation wholly unrelated to my current employment.

Hawkins's position was reminiscent of the campaign aimed at suspected Communists led by Senator Joseph McCarthy and the House Un-American Activities Committee. Targets of the committee were confronted with information from informers, but had no opportunity to cross-examine their accusers and no access to evidence in the possession of the government that would assist their defense. Those who refused to testify by invoking the Fifth Amendment often lost their jobs, were blacklisted, and were ostracized from their communities.

MacDonald was a surly little leprechaun throughout the proceeding. He accused me of "defrauding" the firm and threatened to sue me for getting myself hired under "false pretenses" because I did not tell Hawkins about the Lindh quagmire. (In point of fact, I had told Hawkins when interviewing that I wanted to leave the Justice Department's ethics office because I felt it was not behaving ethically. No one from Hawkins wanted to know the details back then.)

MacDonald then told me in a "Gotcha!" tone of voice that the firm had turned over my computer to the government. Never mind that there was no warrant for it. In an all-too-common over-reading of the Patriot Act, such things were occurring throughout the country with increasing frequency. Never mind that, in turning over my computer, Hawkins willingly gave the government loads of attorney-client privileged communications about other clients. Talk about a massive breach of privilege; ironically, the same thing for which I was being accused. But I'll leave it to Hawkins's clients to be outraged that the firm so willingly gave Uncle Sam privileged communications regarding their private legal matters, which were entirely unrelated to the investigation of me. Finally, MacDonald said menacingly that something "huge" was about to happen in my case. Obviously, the government was still making him big promises.

On March 19, we went to war with Iraq. The film *Wag the Dog*, about a president who fabricated a war to deflect his own failures, had become eerily prophetic. Two days later, Baghdad was flattened in a spectacular day described only and repeatedly as "shock and awe." It was a televised event. The propaganda machine was in overdrive. It was like watching a video game—the viewer is engrossed in it and removed at the same time. It became "all Iraq, all the time" on every major television network. The war bumbled along for more than eight years, ending quietly with no proclamations of victory.

We learned from MacDonald that Agent Powell had done a declaration for the unemployment hearing, which *could* indicate that there was some sort of grand jury activity going on . . . to examine what? Theft of government property for taking copies of my emails, which would not have existed had I not resurrected them from the computer archives? At the US Attorney's Office, Nash had said he'd talk to Rick before "doing anything," but that didn't increase my comfort level. Rick and Mona detected that MacDonald's mood to negotiate seemed to have diminished—he was emboldened by something. MacDonald's "warning" that something big was coming down the pike echoed in my ears. We strategized with Burt Wides about how to let Justice know that Congress was watching, without pushing so hard that the Department would file charges in order to deflect attention off its own conduct and sully my name.

On a bright note, I won the appeal of my unemployment compensation. The hearing officer wrote a great opinion, which rejected the firm's claim that my refusing to talk to the IG was "misconduct" that justified termination of my employment.

Three days later, on March 27, the Justice Department issued an agency-wide gag order in response to a request by Ashcroft. It mandated that employees had to clear any contacts with Congress through Justice's congressional liaison office. This order was in direct contradiction of the First Amendment and various anti-gag statutes. In what was news to me, I learned that Justice had an interagency anti-leak task force, which recommended that government administrators punish employees who leak information. Too bad the anti-leak task force's objectives weren't applied to the "two senior administration officials" from the White House who leaked information that destroyed the career of former ambassador Joseph Wilson's wife, Valerie Plame; or that destroyed the career of Steven Hatfill; or that derailed my career.

A reporter from the *National Law Journal* called Rick and said he thought I was a "hero." But I didn't set out to be a hero and I didn't feel so heroic those days. I was on pins and needles waiting for an indictment to come down.

# SENATOR KENNEDY GROWLS

**M**Y LAW SCHOOL MENTOR, Stephen Bright, put me back in touch with a classmate, Robin Toone, who was now counsel for Senator Kennedy on the Senate Judiciary Committee.

The Pentagon Working Group completed the review it had commenced in mid-January and issued an eighty-five-page report dated April 4, 2003. It made recommendations on what interrogation techniques should be approved. It adopted the reasoning of Bybee's August 2002 memo, noting that, "[d]ue to the unique nature of the war on terrorism . . . the interrogation of unlawful enemy combatants in a manner beyond that which may be applied to a prisoner of war" may be necessary. The next paragraph warned that "[s]hould information regarding the use of more aggressive interrogation techniques . . . become public, it is likely to be exaggerated or distorted in the U.S. and international media accounts, and may produce an adverse effect on support for the war on terrorism." But the US's "coercive interrogation techniques"—code for torture—did not have to be exaggerated or distorted for people to be appalled. They accomplished that all on their own.

Four days later, I got an email from Jill—who had helped me get the job at Hawkins—informing me that the office manager was going to pack up everything in my office. No one had told me I was fired; in fact, three weeks earlier, Plevan had argued at the unemployment hearing that I still worked there.

Mona said it was nothing more than Hawkins continuing to act uncivilized. She asked Plevan if this indirect chatter meant that I had been fired and suggested that Hawkins stop being so circumspect about its adverse employment actions. Plevan asked what we would do about the entire situation, and Mona said I wasn't going to resign because that would cut off my claim to back pay in the lawsuit we were going to bring against them.

Hawkins's lawyer asked if Mona had any other ideas about how to terminate my employment without compromising anyone's rights. Mona suggested that Hawkins call a spade a spade and stop shrugging its shoulders about what my status was: fired. Hawkins's attorney then said that such certainty would prejudice the firm down the road. It was a standoff. By that point, if I still truly "worked" there, the firm owed me five months of back pay. But they really wanted to have it both ways—not to fire me because, in their own words, "it might prejudice them down the road," and not to pay me or let me return to work because it would displease the government.

We weren't to the point yet of really filing a wrongful termination suit. We needed to end the threat of criminal prosecution, which was leaving me hamstrung in terms of a civil action against the Justice Department or Hawkins.

Meanwhile, Rick spoke to Nash of the US Attorney's Office, who was angry about the quote attributed to him in *The New Yorker* about my case not being a high priority. They were, Nash insisted, very interested in it. I thought, *So why don't they* do *something? Anything?* And so what if the quote made the government look ambivalent? It also had to mention the point I was most ashamed of; I was under criminal investigation.

I felt as if I had been placed in legal purgatory with the likes of Steven Hatfill, Wen Ho Lee, and Captain James Yee, where the government had decided I'd done something wrong and was bound and determined to get me. The usual presumption was reversed: You were guilty until proven innocent. The Army arrested Yee—an American citizen, West Point graduate, Muslim convert, and chaplain at the Guantánamo Bay prison—leaked his arrest to the press, smeared him with inflammatory potential charges (sedition, aiding the enemy, spying, and espionage), threw him in solitary confinement for seventy-six days, subjected him to prohibited sleep- and sensory-deprivation techniques, and humiliated him at a pre-court martial hearing. It then dropped all charges against him and put him back on active duty as if nothing had ever happened (except, of course, slapping a gag order on him so that he couldn't talk about the mistreatment). I never could have imagined that seven years later, President Obama would start charging Americans, often whistleblowers, under the Espionage Act as part of his aggressive crackdown on "leaks."

Curiously, Nash asked who was paying my legal fees, a wholly inappropriate question because that information is privileged. Rick suspected that if it had been *Newsweek* or the ACLU, Justice would have been more likely to go after me even harder. That really opened my eyes as to how politicized the whole thing was and how it had nothing to do with the merits of what really happened. It had everything to do with politics—and nothing to do with justice. After I waived the privilege, Rick told Nash that I was paying out of my own pocket, but that we might have to consider getting bankrolled by someone else at some point because it was getting expensive and I had lost my job. Nash said he was well aware of my employment situation.

Of course he was. The Justice Department had orchestrated it.

Rick suggested to Nash that someone at Justice should focus on the substance of what was in *The New Yorker*. Apparently, a lot of people at the Department were doing just that—but their goal was to shut me up, not find out what really happened.

Rumsfeld, acting on the Pentagon Working Group's recommendation, reissued his guidance for Guantánamo Bay on April 16, 2003. He sent General Hill a memo approving twenty-four interrogation techniques, four of which were considered harsh enough to require Rumsfeld's explicit approval. Forced nudity (in Bush-speak, "removal of clothing"), while earlier approved for use at Guantánamo Bay, was not among the authorized techniques in his revised guidelines, but at least five of the other modified high-pressure tactics were later listed in an October 9 memo governing Abu Ghraib, the prison that came to symbolize American torture.

As the major combat ended in Iraq (or so we were led to believe), I served on federal jury duty. No one questioned my patriotism for that onerous civic task. I'm only unpatriotic when it suits the government's interests.

I continued writing, as a way of trying to process what happened in the Lindh case, what was happening to me, and, on a larger scale, what was happening to our country. Another law review article of mine was accepted by the *William & Mary Bill of Rights Journal*, this one entitled "United States Citizens Detained as 'Enemy Combatants': The Right to Counsel as a Matter of Ethics." New breath was given to the statement that the personal is political, an oft-repeated if incompletely understood slogan at college. But I did not write about my own experience; rather, I wrote about enemy combatants and government whistleblowers as a purely academic matter. It was safe that way. It was a cathartic outlet in the highbrow genre of legal academia and it was an initial step toward rehabilitating my reputation as an expert in legal ethics, which the government was trying not only to downplay, but to dispute. If I could intellectualize it, perhaps I could understand it.

I was invited to teach a class at my alma mater, Yale Law School, which was uplifting, and I received a warm reception. Professor Owen Fiss, whom I never had as a teacher, was very complimentary and gave me a heartfelt and flattering introduction. He had read my enemy combatant paper with resounding approval. I felt as if I had a lot of intelligent things to say during the question-and-answer period and had developed an expertise that I could share with the students. "We take care of our own," one of the deans reminded me, but it was never to be a full-throated embrace, the way it was with my some of my classmates, who were doing great—but uncontroversial—things.

The following week I gave a speech before the Philadelphia Bar Association, which honored me:

> . . . for her conduct as a lawyer, at great expense to her personal career. Not only should she be honored for behaving at the highest professional standards, but our commending her in a public way may call attention to the very highhanded and unfair predicament in which she now finds herself.

It felt nice to be validated, rather than vilified. My speech was well received, and it gave me hope to be embraced by at least a tiny portion of the legal community. It meant the world to me during that lonely time.

NBC World News Tonight featured an FBI whistleblower, Jane Turner, who reported the theft of a globe from Ground Zero. She received the predictable scathing performance evaluation, which sounded a lot like mine. The government was shooting the messenger, rather than addressing the message by investigating the underlying misconduct about which she complained.

The Justice Department, to which the FBI reports, gained quite a reputation for its retaliation against whistleblowers. After John Roberts, a unit chief in the FBI's Office of Professional Responsibility, discussed FBI shortcomings with "60 Minutes," his supervisor disciplined him. After FBI translator Sibel Edmonds complained to her supervisor about poor management, slow progress, incompetence, and corruption, she was fired. The Justice Department invoked the rarely used, but increasingly popular, "state secrets privilege" to prevent her from providing evidence and retroactively classified testimony by FBI officials that corroborated her story. The agency also retaliated against former FBI agent Mike German, an undercover specialist, for complaining about a botched anti-terrorism investigation. Following in Coleen Rowley's footsteps, Sibel, Mike, and I all eventually went on to become whistleblower advocates within the civil liberties and good-government community.

My case, meanwhile, grew stagnant. It appeared that it was, in fact, "on the back burner." Metaphorically comparing the Justice Department with a sleeping bear, did we really want to poke it? We had already disturbed it once with *The New Yorker* article.

The decision about whether to grant press interviews was soon made for me during a surreal month from May to June 2003 during which I became embroiled in the confirmation hearing of Michael Chertoff, the assistant attorney general for the Justice Department's Criminal Division. He was nominated to be a judge on the Third Circuit Court of Appeals and was considered a relatively vanilla Republican compared to judicial nominees such as Janice Rogers Brown, Pricilla Owen, Charles Pickering, William Pryor, and Carolyn Kuhl.

Chertoff's intellectual prowess made him the inspiration for an intense and brilliant character in his classmate Scott Turow's bestselling book, *One L*, about their days as first-year students at Harvard Law School. He made his name prosecuting Fat Tony Salerno, the mobster and a former Genovese family boss, and Crazy Eddie, the once-ubiquitous electronics retailer, who referred to him as "Count Chertoff."

In a more embarrassing chapter of Chertoff's otherwise storied career, he had worked as special counsel to the Senate committee that investigated the Whitewater affair and gave serious consideration to wild Clinton conspiracy theories. He had previously cultivated an apolitical reputation, but Whitewater marked his emergence as a staunch Republican, which ultimately won him an important future patron in then-Senator Ashcroft. (Chertoff eventually became the first director of the Nazi-sounding Homeland Security Department. Today, he and Ashcroft work together as principals in a consulting organization that epitomizes DC's revolving door between government and the private sector, the Chertoff Group, which represents the manufacturer of the soft-porn full-body scanners at airports.)

Chertoff's office at the Justice Department had now become terror central. It was at the middle of the most important criminal investigation in American history: 9/11. He had been the senior Justice official on duty at the FBI command center when the terrorist attacks occurred.

In early May, Senator Kennedy asked Chertoff about the Lindh interrogation during Chertoff's nomination hearing. Chertoff, incredibly, denied that PRAO ever took a position on the Lindh interrogation, a brazen assertion considering that the public record contradicted his denial. "I have to say, Senator, I think that the Professional Responsibility [Advisory] Office was never asked for advice in this matter. I was involved in it."

Chertoff couldn't stop himself from embellishing. "Mr. Lindh was Mirandized, and had he requested counsel or requested to invoke his right to silence at the point at which the FBI was involved, they would have honored the request." I had to admit it was impressive that he could pack so many distortions into a single sentence. The second part of his statement was, at best, a gross mischaracterization of what happened and, at worst, perjury. As Jane Mayer's uncontroverted article documented, "[FBI Agent] Reimann read Lindh the Miranda warning. But, when noting the right to counsel, the agent now acknowledges, he ad-libbed, 'Of course there are no lawyers here.'"

Senator Kennedy asked Chertoff a second time, "[D]o you remember what the Professional Responsibility Advisory Office['s] . . . position was on this?"

"I was not consulted with respect to this matter," Chertoff answered. "There are other parts of the Department that generally render opinions in this area of the law and other expertise that was consulted." More dodging and obfuscation.

Kennedy tenaciously persevered. "Well, your statement that the Professional Responsibility Advisory Office did not have an official position on this—"

"I don't believe they have an official position on this," Chertoff interrupted.

Years later, when I obtained a copy of the IG leak report, it revealed that Chertoff *did* know that a Department attorney he supervised, De Pue, sought PRAO's advice.

According to the IG leak report, De Pue's superiors were upset that he had sought PRAO's advice about Lindh's questioning. According to De Pue's sworn statement to the IG, "[A supervisor] informed me that the criminal division's leadership was disturbed that I had sought PRAO's advice in this matter." Eric Lichtblau of the *New York Times* got De Pue to go on the record that "[t]he front office was unhappy with my inquiry. I was more or less told that I was out of line in making that inquiry. It was not a popular thing to do, but I thought at the time it was the reasonable thing to do . . ." According to the article, De Pue understood the displeasure as coming from Chertoff. I was grateful to De Pue for his honesty, and sorry to learn that he, too, had suffered negative repercussions for trying to follow the rules.

I suggested to Robin Toone that Kennedy question Chertoff about whether Chertoff was part of the decision to conceal Judge Ellis' discovery order from me. I also suggested that Kennedy might want to ask whether or not Claudia Flynn was ever investigated for not telling me (an attorney under her direct supervision) that there was a federal court order that covered my emails. Heck, why not ask Chertoff whether he was concerned that the *ethics* office had been accused of behaving in an entirely unethical manner, including destroying evidence and obstructing justice. I was seething that Chertoff was going to effortlessly lie his way into a federal judgeship.

I met with Eric Lichtblau of the *New York Times* and Douglas McCollam of *The American Lawyer*, followed by a Mother's Day tea at Jacob's school. They served us drinks and cake and sang a sweet song:

> Inch by inch, row by row,
> We're gonna make this garden grow
> All it takes is a rake and a hoe
> And a piece of fertile ground.
>
> Inch by inch, row by row
> Someone bless these seeds I sow . . .

Two days later, I learned I was pregnant.

Meanwhile, Senator Kennedy submitted written follow-up questions to Chertoff. I was incredulous that, this time around, Chertoff lied *in writing* and that he didn't seize the opportunity to massage, clarify, or revise his earlier answers. One of the written questions asked how the emails in *Newsweek* were consistent with Chertoff's position that PRAO never took a position on Lindh's interrogation.

Chertoff repeated, again, that:

> [T]hose at the Department responsible for the Lindh matter before and during the time of Lindh's interrogations did not to my knowledge seek PRAO's advice. I am not aware that PRAO ever took an official position about the Lindh interrogation or that any views expressed by an individual PRAO attorney were documented, factually and legally substantiated, reviewed and authorized, as I would expect before an official opinion was rendered. The email traffic that you cite appears to be the impressions of a single PRAO attorney, without any factual analysis and case law discussion, and therefore would not constitute an official opinion.

Chertoff had clearly started to lay the groundwork for dismissing PRAO's advice. He denied knowledge that PRAO's advice was sought, but then, apparently as a fallback position, preemptively discounted any advice that came from a "single individual" (such as me), saying that it would not be "an official position" that comports with his understanding of how "an official opinion" is rendered. He dismissed the email traffic as merely a lone attorney's legally inadequate fanciful musings—as if I just went around spouting off unsolicited ethics advice for fun.

I knew that it would come to this: a personal attack. However, no amount of bracing for a punch can ever really prepare you for the hit.

Senator Kennedy next asked about my being extorted out of my job with the bogus performance evaluation. Chertoff conveniently denied having any knowledge about my employment, performance, or departure.

"Has any investigation been conducted into the alleged withholding of emails from the federal court in the Lindh case?" Kennedy asked. "Was Claudia J. Flynn, Director of PRAO, investigated in relation to these events? Have any Justice Department employees other than Ms. Radack been reprimanded or disciplined in any way?" I wanted to hug Kennedy. Not only was he fearless when it came to the Justice Department, he demanded accountability.

"It would be improper for me to comment on whether or not Ms. Flynn was investigated," Chertoff responded, citing a provision of the US Attorney's Manual, which his office had studiously ignored for the past year and a half. Despite Chertoff's slick answer, Kennedy was relentless.

"Is Ms. Radack the target of a criminal investigation by the US Attorney's Office? For what is she being investigated?" Kennedy asked.

Chertoff again cited a provision of the US Attorney's Manual and said that it would be improper for him to comment on whether I was under investigation and, if so, about what my status might be. I found this completely laughable because, while Chertoff claimed with a straight face that it would be improper for him to tell the Senate Judiciary Committee whether I was under investigation, the Department of Justice felt perfectly comfortable sharing this sensitive information with my private law firm.

In the icing on the cake of Chertoff's "testilying," he stated erroneously that because a law enforcement agent, not a lawyer, had interrogated Lindh, then no attorney could be implicated. This faulty reasoning emerged again in the Abu Ghraib scandal and again in Chertoff's confirmation hearing to head the Department of Homeland Security. Attorney ethics rules state that a lawyer should be held responsible for the conduct and activities of agents or investigators acting on the lawyer's behalf or who are associated with the lawyer. No wonder Rumsfeld wanted to cut lawyers out of the loop. He mocked us as worrywart bureaucrats and nitpickers and resented the "legalistic hurdles" (like the Constitution) that got in the way of doing what he wanted. "Reduce the number of lawyers," he said. "They are like beavers—they get in the middle of the stream and dam it up."

Chertoff's nomination was held over for another week because Kennedy wanted to submit even more questions.

The *New York Times* ran an article by Lichtblau, the headline of which read "Dispute Over Legal Advice Costs a Job and Complicates a Nomination." Kennedy was quoted in the article as saying, "I'm very concerned about this Radack situation." My husband, a Massachusetts native, cut out the quote, enlarged it, and put it up at work.

The controversy culminated in a contentious Senate Judiciary hearing in which the Committee voted 13-0, with all six Democrats effectively abstaining, to send Chertoff's nomination to the full Senate for consideration.

Democrats requested a second delay in the vote on Chertoff, which angered Senator Orrin Hatch, chairman of the Senate Judiciary Committee, who attacked Lichtblau for his article and the delay it had caused in voting on Chertoff. Hatch claimed that the article was an unfair effort to "smear this acclaimed public servant," Chertoff, even though the article was about the Justice Department smearing me. "It's disgraceful at this last minute the *New York Times* is attempting to impugn anybody," Hatch said. "Lichtblau shared bylines with the infamous Mr. Blair," the *Times* reporter who had recently resigned for fabricating stories. Talk about unfairly impugning someone.

Senator Kennedy, in a moving and strongly worded public statement on the nomination, expressed his dissatisfaction with Chertoff's elliptical answers:

Last week I expressed my concern about Mr. Chertoff's failure to provide serious, consistent, and responsible answers to the questions asked by a member of this Committee. In particular, his answers to my first set of written questions were non-responsive, evasive, and hyper-technical. They were stingy in substance, avoiding the questions that were asked, and often answering questions that were not asked . . . Evasive and non-responsive answers will not do—no matter how "uncontroversial" a nomination may otherwise be.

Though it received little play in the press, Kennedy's statement about Chertoff's misleading answers spoke volumes. Even though Kennedy ultimately supported Chertoff's nomination, as I knew all along that he would, it was still extremely gratifying to have Chertoff called out on the carpet.

On June 9, 2003, Chertoff was confirmed. It galled me that Chertoff would now sit in judgment of others and make $167,000 a year for doing it. I only hoped that those who appeared before him would take their oath to tell the truth more seriously than Chertoff took his.

# THE SWORD OF DAMOCLES

STARTED TO RECEIVE WARNINGS from a number of reporters that one of my former co-workers at PRAO, Joan Goldfrank, was reaching out to them and trashing me. Joan became the self-appointed attack dog, taking it upon herself to contact reporters whenever she learned there was an article on my situation in the works, and even after an article was published. It appears that whenever Claudia was called for comment, she would immediately hand it off to Joan, the unofficial opposition spokesperson.

Joan told reporters that my husband basically "left me," neglecting to tell them that he worked for the World Bank and went on long travel assignments. She said I wrote men's names on a so-called "Rape List" at Brown University, rather than the fact that I worked on reform of sexual harassment and assault policy during college. She even went so far as to say that *I* was the obstructer in the Lindh case. According to her twisted fantasy, I removed the emails from the PRAO file. What earthly reason would I have to remove the emails, unhesitatingly highlight such a dastardly act, go to such great lengths to resurrect the emails, and throw away my career to expose them?

Joan, however, didn't realize the significance of her accusation: It was the first time anyone who had been at PRAO *admitted* that the emails were missing from the file. The Department never denied this fact, but it had never confirmed it either. Instead, Justice's position seemed to be that since at least some of the emails eventually reached the court (we'll never know for sure how many because the Justice Department has strenuously resisted unsealing the "documents" they claim to be my emails), then no harm, no foul.

Joan's behavior was actually textbook retaliation against whistle-blowers: smears of purported misconduct similar to what the employee was alleging. In my case, the smear included accusing me of unethical conduct—purging the file when *they* in fact had done the purging and breaching attorney-client privilege when *they* were the ones who had abused it and committed illegal acts under its cover. Joan failed to realize that digging up dirt on your accuser is widely viewed not as part of your defense, but as indicative that you have none.

I think part of Joan's strategy was to sling mud at me just to make me have to deny it. It reminded me of Lyndon Johnson's anecdote about an old Texas congressman who once falsely accused an opponent of having sex with sheep, just to make the man deny it. Joan started all sorts of ugly rumors, just to make me have to deny them. Rick eventually had to send her a "cease and desist" letter because her defamation had reached such extremes. But she couldn't help herself. Eight years later, the stale, unresolved bar complaint arising from my ordeal suddenly sprang to life as I was at the height of successfully defending a whistleblower in a high-profile prosecution by the Justice Department, which was collapsing by the hour. The DC Bar abruptly awoke from its long slumber and presented me with a Statement of Charges, nearly a decade in the making, in which Joan Goldfrank had changed from being a bit player to the star witness against me. It was total déjà vu and so clearly politically motivated.

Gregg Leslie, an acquaintance from the Reporters' Committee for Freedom of the Press, buttonholed Isikoff at a journalists' conference and asked him if he was concerned about how I was being treated. According to Leslie, Isikoff was not concerned. Isikoff said that the Department of Justice was just trying to scare me—as if that were okay; as if *that*—the US government terrorizing one of its own citizens—were not a story.

As of the summer of 2003, Hawkins still had me listed as an associate on Martindale Hubbell (a database of lawyers and law firms), kept my voice mail activated, and called me at home to give me personal messages. They wouldn't pay me and wouldn't allow me to come to work, yet they told *The American Lawyer* magazine that I was still employed by them—just on something akin to "medical leave." They neglected to mention that medical leave, unlike the black hole I was in, was voluntary, often entailed some kind of compensation, and guaranteed you a place when you returned. Imperfect analogies aside, Hawkins wouldn't admit the truth: The government was leaning on them heavily to get rid of me and they didn't want to get on the wrong side of the government.

*The American Lawyer* reporter, Douglas McCollam, discovered that all the calls the government traced were from Isikoff to me, which prompted Isikoff to worry that his phone was being tapped. Isikoff wanted to see the "evidence" that MacDonald presented to us, courtesy of the US government. I grudgingly obliged, though I certainly didn't feel like I owed him any favors.

The press is a strange animal, and I say that as both a popular blogger and a freelance writer for the mainstream media. The "Fourth Estate" can bring transparency to government agencies, shape public opinion, and level the playing field. Investigative reporting can take disputes out of the stifling secrecy of government agencies and into the glare of public scrutiny. Media coverage can transform a workplace "troublemaker" into a public hero and reduce a supervisory official to a beleaguered figure whose resignation is demanded, or at least disempower a rogue office.

But the media can also try to make a story of the whistleblower. (In a hurtful smear piece for *Mother Jones*, I was described as a "moral narcissist" by an "expert" who'd never met me.) Reporters like to add drama to their stories and the tortured whistleblower angle is ripe for exploitation.

Media exposure can also further inflame the agency against you as it finds itself on the defensive in an embarrassing public forum. Every article on me seemed to enrage the political appointees at the Justice Department and always provoked some sort of retaliatory response. It was like waking the sleeping giant.

This was exacerbated by an unavoidable tendency for reporters to want to "try the case" in the media. And a story's effects can be evanescent, particularly in this age of short attention spans and news cycles that change at lightning speed. New distractions manufactured by the person on whom you're blowing the whistle can steal the public's attention. The Bush administration was especially adept at this bait-and-switch routine.

Most laypersons are not schooled in knowing a reporter's "beat," creating a "hook" for the story without having it buried in their own back, laying "ground rules," going "off the record," or speaking "on background." I believe journalists have a duty to educate sources at least minimally. Isikoff did not; in fact, he asked if I wanted to be quoted in the article.

"Won't that identify me as the source?" I asked.

"Yeah, probably," he said. He should have volunteered this near-certainty. He didn't let me know that the information alone would reveal me as the probable source. Although I chose not to be quoted because I wanted to blow the whistle anonymously—this was not about fame, greed, or personal ambition—I was not told that my emails would be published in full, including my name, on the magazine's website. He did not warn me that I should not take his calls at work (and he should not have called me at work).

I turned down the majority of media requests, and only agreed to print media over which I had more control, not broadcast media such as TV or radio. It is hard to constantly push the spotlight on the issue and off of yourself. People usually leak anonymously, as I did (and as one of my eventual clients, Thomas Drake, did), so the media will focus on the message without exposing, or getting distracted by, the messenger. But can the media really deliver the message and not the messenger? Anytime someone did an article, I had severe publication anxiety. It stressed me to the core to continually have to clarify, rebut, and confirm what other people said. It was exhausting.

Today I still have a cautious relationship with reporters, but see them as the best mechanism for accountability. Most have done unspeakable good and only two have hurt me and hurt the public's right to know what their government was doing, even if unintentionally. Media coverage never had the surefire "bullet proofing" effect of deterring the Justice Department from attacking me. But the media—especially investigative journalists Jane Mayer and Eric Lichtblau—did ferret out the truth from a secretive, locked-down, powerful, and vengeful Justice Department. And truth is an incredible gift. By and large, the media has been the saving grace of whistleblowers, and this guided my strategy in future cases of the whistleblowers I went on to represent.

Strange bedfellows have been a recurring phenomenon throughout my saga, so it was serendipitous but not shocking that Bruce Fein came into my life, just like one of those deeply appreciated surprises when Jane Mayer showed up on my doorstep and when Senator Kennedy took up my cause. My uncle, Al Guttman, is a real estate lawyer. One of his tenants was the legendary constitutional law expert Bruce Fein, and my uncle kept urging me to meet him.

A top-level Justice Department official in the Reagan administration, he was known for his conservative credentials, so I really did not think he would take an interest in my case, which seemed so ideologically driven. (I had no way of knowing, nor would I have ever imagined, that in the future, President Obama would treat whistleblowers even worse than Bush did.)

My uncle arranged a lunch for the three of us in July. Bruce is brilliant in the way only a few people in my classes at Brown University and Yale Law School were; not just book-smart, but truly dazzling. He's lanky, pale, boyish, and unimposing. I think I weigh more than Bruce even when I'm not pregnant. He possesses an encyclopedic knowledge of history, a mastery of the classics, and has a Rolodex deeper than the Pacific Ocean. How he speaks is how I imagine James Madison would sound. Yet I was struck by his modesty, openness, and compassion—emotional traits often lacking in people so cerebral.

We had lunch and spoke easily for hours. He was familiar with my case and said he wanted to represent me. He favored taking a more aggressive approach in bringing this whole debacle to a close, for example, by seeking a letter clearing me. I was not optimistic because, as a Justice attorney, I knew first-hand that government investigations were notorious for dragging on for years and that they rarely did you the courtesy of letting you know when the case was closed. A letter actually clearing you was virtually unheard of. Bruce believed that the only person ever to have received such a letter was Clark Clifford, the key advisor to four presidents who was indicted on the basis of a Manhattan D.A.'s speculative and novel theory that two separate legal transactions somehow constituted a conspiracy of fraud and bribery.

Bruce's approach differed from Rick Robinson's "lay low" approach and he was more inclined to go on the offensive and to use the media. In the words of Supreme Court Justice Louis Brandeis's elegant axiom, "Sunlight is the best disinfectant," and illumination has proven to be a cure (or at least a neutralizing force) for the Bush administration's skewering of those who speak the truth. I told Bruce I'd have to run it by Rick, with whom Bruce was totally willing to coordinate and cooperate. I was just concerned about offending Rick because he might think I was shopping my case to another lawyer, which was not my intent in meeting Bruce. I was also concerned about incurring even more legal bills, which was enough, in and of itself, to make me nearly reject the idea out of hand.

Luckily, Rick and Bruce behaved as dignified adults rather than territorial egomaniacs. Lawyers don't seem to play well together as a general rule, but Rick was not upset that I'd met with Bruce and said he was not adverse to working with him. At the end of July, they had lunch and decided that Bruce would co-represent me. Moreover, Bruce was willing to do so pro bono, meaning free of charge! This was fantastic news and a welcome peak on my emotional roller coaster.

Bruce is a pure libertarian. Ashcroft used to be aligned with the civil libertarian wing of the conservative movement—those who opposed expanding the federal government. In a 1997 op-ed piece, Ashcroft criticized government attempts to monitor the Internet to combat crime: "We do not provide the government with phone jacks outside our homes for unlimited wiretaps. Why, then, should we grant government the Orwellian capability to listen at will and in real-time to our communications across the Web?" His own words are the best illustration of the hypocrisy (never mind the illegality) of the domestic warrantless wiretapping program that Lichtblau and his colleague, James Risen, later revealed in a *New York Times* article that unleashed one of the biggest scandals of the Bush administration. I still didn't fully appreciate that I had gotten caught up in the embryonic stages of the Bush administration's other big scandal: torture.

After September 11, Ashcroft acted more authoritarian than libertarian. Once a critic of expanding federal law enforcement power, he now argued that the administration could be "trusted" to exercise wide power with no questions asked. Seven years later, the *Washington Post* ran an investigative series on how "[t]he top-secret world the government created in response to the terrorist attacks on Sept. 11, 2011, has become so unwieldy and so secretive that no one knows how much money it costs, how many people it employs, how many programs exist within it or exactly how many agencies do the same work." Ashcroft was no longer against big government. He just had his own vision of what it should look like. Conservatives who were once identified with protecting individual rights against the unchecked power of the government now claimed that the Commander-in-Chief was above the law and that the ends justified the means.

Bruce fervently believed that what happened to me hindered the free flow of information about government operations both within the government and to the public. "The Justice Department is going to end up like the Politburo," he was fond of saying, "with underlings telling superiors only what they want to hear."

The government is hiding what is occurring behind closed doors in what are supposed to be *public* agencies. The Patriot Act inverted the traditional public-private paradigm, whereby people's lives were private and the work of the government was public. It created a new structure that makes our inner lives open books and the workings of the government opaque. A fundamental precept of our system is that the business of "the people" should be conducted so that the citizenry knows what is being done in its name. Instead, the Bush administration shut down court proceedings with the rare "state-secrets privilege," obsessively over-classified documents, used secret "signing statements" to modify the meaning of laws, and hermetically sealed the way agencies conduct the public's business. And truth-tellers who shine the light on government corruption are increasingly punished unmercifully in a very public way.

Bruce was determined to remove the "Sword of Damocles" that was dangling precariously over my head. The allusion comes from the myth of Dionysius, the fourth century BC tyrant of Syracuse. To all appearances, he was very rich and comfortable, enjoying all the luxuries that money and power could buy. He even had court flatterers to stroke his ego. One of them was Damocles. Damocles used to make gratuitous comments to the king about his wealth and lavish life. One day when Damocles complimented the tyrant on his abundance and power, Dionysius turned to Damocles and asked, "If you think I'm so lucky, how would you like to try out my life?"

Damocles readily agreed, and so Dionysius invited him to a banquet at which he got to sit at Dionysius's throne. Damocles was enjoying himself immensely until he noticed a sharp sword above his head, which was suspended from the ceiling by a single horsehair. This, Dionysius explained to Damocles, was what the insecure life of a ruler was really like. Damocles quickly revised his idea of what made for a good life and eagerly returned to his poorer but safer existence.

The Department's investigation was indeed a sword hanging over my head.

Bruce drafted a "Motion to Inspect" the secret leak report that was being used against me, but to which I had no access. It was my first chance to tell my side of the story, exactly my way. Judge Ellis would finally hear my version of events and would learn of the government's abuse of both his February discovery order and his June order calling for a three-week leak investigation, which the government used as a pretext to make my life miserable for a period of years. It all would be documented in a public court filing for the world to see. Forget

Claudia Flynn and Joan Goldfrank. Who was I protecting? Why did I still retain any allegiance whatsoever to my former office? I guess it's because I still wanted to believe that the government is fundamentally good. But there seemed to be no downside to telling my side. I named names and spelled out in vivid detail who did what and when they did it. It was a liberating act, whether the motion was granted or not.

A DC law firm began courting me aggressively to join them. A partner there said they didn't give a damn about the government's investigation of me, that they were willing to let me work my own hours, and that they were defending people similarly situated to me. It sounded like the perfect job opportunity. They asked me to come up with my ideal job schedule.

During this time, I was also invited by the ABA Task Force on Treatment of Enemy Combatants to help draft its proposal to set minimum standards for civilian defense counsel representing alleged terrorists before military commissions. At the ABA's policy-setting House of Delegates' annual meeting, the ABA passed the Military Commission Recommendation and Report overwhelmingly with no debate. I felt as if my life was getting back on track.

In late August 2003, the Joint Staff in the Pentagon sent General Miller—who was then commander of detention operations at Guantánamo—to Iraq to assist in the startup of the Abu Ghraib prison. He was accompanied by a retinue of senior aides from Guantánamo, including officials from the CIA and the Defense Intelligence Agency. Miller brought with him Guantánamo interrogation techniques, which appeared in the form of forcing a detainee named Mohammed al-Qahtani to wear a leash, perform dog tricks, and wear women's underwear.

As the second anniversary of September 11 approached, the White House kept trying to link 9/11 to Iraq, as if Sadaam Hussein was somehow working with al Qaeda, a position Bush continued to assert even after the 9/11 Commission disproved it. Shortly after Miller completed his inspection of the Abu Ghraib jail, he departed Iraq on September 9 and returned to brief Pentagon officials on his ideas for "Gitmo-izing" Iraq.

Miller presented his interrogation rules to Lieutenant General Ricardo Sanchez, who was then the senior US military commander in Iraq. On the eve of September 11, Sanchez personally approved an "Interrogation and Counter-Resistance Policy," which contained a series of "coercive interrogation techniques," many of which went beyond the limits set in the Army's field manual and were outlawed by the Geneva Conventions.

No formalized rules for interrogation existed in Iraq before the policy imposed that day. Sanchez borrowed heavily from the infamous list of high-pressure interrogation tactics used at the detention facility in Guantánamo Bay. He approved letting guards at Abu Ghraib use military dogs, temperature extremes, reversed sleep patterns, sensory deprivation, and starvation on detainees whenever they wished. The thirty-two interrogation tactics could be imposed without first seeking the approval of anyone outside the prison.

Soon after, a videotape of bin Laden was aired. It was chilling to see him in the flesh.

# DEATH BY A THOUSAND PAPER CUTS

**M**Y GOAL ON THE SECOND ANNIVERSARY of 9/11, as I'm sure it was for many people, was just to make it through the day. This day represented not only the grief and loss that everyone in our country was feeling, but for me personally, a loss of the daily way of life I had known—the loss of two jobs, privacy, friends (certain ones), reputation, financial security, confidence, and peace of mind. Now our country was operating under the "Ashcroft Doctrine," "Bush Justice," the unitary executive theory, and the very undemocratic Patriot Act that our country reflexively renews and expands.

I muddled through the day, spending a lot of time remembering, thinking, reflecting, and mourning. Someone we knew from this area, Linda C. Lee, had died in the Trade Center's elegant restaurant, Windows on the World. She was only thirty-four. A senior associate at Jennison Associates, a financial services firm, she had been attending a technology conference at the World Trade Center when a plane struck the first tower, shutting her up in a sepulcher in the sky. I lit a *yahrzeit* candle to commemorate the anniversary of her death. Jews

121

believe that the soul of the departed derives joy from the kindling of lights. Her soul is God's candle.

At the end of the day, Rick shook me from my ruminations. He told me that Nash called him from the US Attorney's Office and said the criminal case was closed and that they no longer had an active investigation.

I was just stunned. No explanation was offered as to why, why *now*, what they were ever going to charge me with in the first place, or what made them decide not to. I have my hunches, of course. There was a lot going on in the atmospherics; the *New York Times* was about to publish a sympathetic story on my situation, which the dropping of the investigation effectively killed because (in the words of the editor) "her life is no longer being held hostage." Bruce Fein had been shopping around to various media outlets the "Motion to Inspect" the secret leak report to see if they wanted to sign on as petitioners. He was sure that the Justice Department had gotten wind of it. Ashcroft had just wrapped up his dog-and-pony show touting the Patriot Act (a month earlier, he set out on a publicity blitz in which he stumped for the Act in thirty-two cities in more than twenty states, including election "swing" states), and President Bush had just endorsed the proposed Patriot Act II. I was on congressional lists to testify against it.

Or perhaps it was something simpler. John Richter, the Chief of Staff for the Justice Department's Criminal Division (and later its acting assistant attorney general) came to a block party my family hosted and saw that I wasn't such a pariah after all. Our kids jumped together on the Moon Bounce in my front yard as his wife tended to their daughter in our kitchen. Anyway, I'll never know for sure why the case was dropped. What I *do* know for sure is that the government never meaningfully investigated the underlying issue of the cover-up I exposed; however, through hard-hitting investigative journalism,

Jane Mayer's *The Dark Side* and Eric Lichtblau's *Bush's Law* basically solved the mystery.

"As quickly as it began, it ended," my husband said. I'd like to say we were both relieved, but neither of us had any trust in the government's word. The next step would be for Rick to send the prosecutor something memorializing their conversation because we were never going to get a letter clearing me. I'd like to say we celebrated, but it's impossible to really celebrate anything on 9/11. We went to Bob's Famous Ice Cream and ate cotton candy sherbet in relative silence with our kids. It was a quiet acknowledgment, but the main thing I felt was loss.

Everyone thought my ordeal was over when the criminal investigation ended, just as they had when the Lindh case crumbled. All I had to do was start picking up the broken pieces of my life—no small task, but at least I could move forward. How naïve I was to think that this vindictive administration was through with me.

The dropping of the criminal case strengthened our "Motion to Inspect" because the government could no longer argue that unsealing the secret leak report would interfere with an ongoing investigation. There was no longer any conceivable reason to keep the report under seal. Mona also favored filing the motion because it could reveal the extent to which Hawkins acted as the alter ego of the government.

At the end of September, Rick asked the Justice Department whether its Office of Professional Responsibility was conducting an investigation into my whistleblower allegations, as the *New York Times* had reported back during the Chertoff proceedings.

I had been out of work for nearly a year and was hopeful that I could get a job. But those hopes were dashed on October 1, 2003, when I was surprisingly rejected by the law firm that had courted me. Despite their bravado, it turns out that they were just as cowardly as the rest. They didn't even have the courage or the courtesy to call me. Instead, I received an email:

> You're obviously a very capable attorney. But accusations about you, however unfounded, could complicate [your representation of our clients.] . . . The very public nature . . . would lead to media scrutiny . . . The risks here are too great.

At least they were honest about why I was being dinged.

The High Holy Days were upon us again. The rabbi implored, "Keep my tongue from evil . . . Help me be silent in the face of derision." I felt very conflicted. Why should I remain silent when people were smearing me? This whole ordeal happened because I refused to keep silent in the face of wrongdoing.

The service on the eve of Yom Kippur reminded me that "for transgressions of one human being against another, the Day of Atonement does not atone until they have made peace with one another." I was not holding my breath that anyone would seek my forgiveness or try to make amends with me. So I instead focused on the passage that dealt with my responsibility of forgiving all who had hurt me, all who had wronged me, "whether deliberately or inadvertently, whether by word or by deed." Claudia Flynn, Joan Goldfrank, Ron Powell, Glenn Fine, Cullen MacDonald, Michael Chertoff; it was a long list and none of them, at least half of whom are Jewish, sought *my* forgiveness. Not that I expected them to; apologizing was not a forte of the Bush administration.

The rabbi's sermon dealt with enemy combatants, xenophobia, and the evils of the Patriot Act. I felt as if it had been custom written for me. For once, I didn't feel like the black sheep of the flock. I sent Rabbi Reiner my latest law review article on enemy combatants and confided in him my situation. He immediately called me at home. I explained my dilemma in forgiving the Bush cabal. He said that seeking justice was different than seeking forgiveness.

An October 9 memo on "Interrogation Rules of Engagement," which each military intelligence officer at Abu Ghraib was asked to sign, set out in detail the wide range of pressure tactics approved in September and available before the rules were changed on October 12. The Guantánamo rules were the template for the rules put into place at Abu Ghraib. While it stated that "at no time will detainees be treated inhumanely nor maliciously humiliated," it permitted the use of yelling, loud music, temperature extremes, and "stress positions" for as long as forty-five minutes every four hours—all without first obtaining the permission of anyone more senior than the interrogation officer in charge at Abu Ghraib. At Guantánamo, interrogators needed approval from a two-star general (at least in theory) before they could use tactics such as isolating prisoners, reversing their sleep patterns, or denying them food. Although the October 9 Abu Ghraib memo called attention to the strictures of the Uniform Code of Military Justice, it never quoted from it.

Officials at the Florida headquarters of the US Central Command, which has overall military responsibility for Iraq, objected to some of the interrogation tactics approved by Sanchez in September, including the more severe methods that he had said could be used at any time at Abu Ghraib with the consent of the interrogation officer in charge. On October 12, Sanchez decided to remove several items on his list and to require that prison officials obtain his direct approval for the remaining high-pressure methods. Among the tactics supposedly dropped were those that would take away prisoners' religious items, that controlled their exposure to light, and that allowed interrogators to pretend to be from a country that tortures prisoners.

The high-pressure options that remained included taking someone to a miserable location for interrogation, diet manipulation, prolonged isolation, using military dogs to provoke fear, and imposing "stress positions" for as long as forty-five minutes. Sanchez did not drop those tactics until May 2004, when the twisted photographs of Abu Ghraib detainees were published.

Even though the list of high-pressure interrogation options was truncated on October 12, a number of military personnel did not get the memo, literally. The use of stress positions and military dogs to intimidate prisoners were used at Abu Ghraib as late as January of 2004. Six months later we would see photos of these rule violations made manifest in the most grotesque and graphic ways. Pentagon officials said such tactics shouldn't have been approved under any circumstances.

Toward the end of October, when I flew to a family function in New Mexico, I was pulled aside during passenger screening for a more extensive search than the usual stroll through the magnetometer. I didn't think twice about it. I remembered Israeli security forces arresting a young Palestinian who was planning to disguise herself as a pregnant woman, with a bomb hidden beneath her falsely enlarged belly. It made sense that my being seven-months pregnant might raise suspicions.

I returned home to a letter from the Justice Department's Office of Professional Responsibility. They acknowledged the receipt of Rick's letter at the end of September, in which he inquired about whether they were conducting an investigation of my whistleblower allegations.

The next paragraph blindsided me: "Please be advised that we have referred Ms. Radack to the bar [disciplinary authorities] of the District of Columbia and Maryland, of which we understand she is a member." They were now going after my law license.

They also wrote, laughably, "We take allegations of misconduct by Department personnel very seriously and we are investigating Ms. Radack's allegations." They admitted that they had been aware of my allegations for nearly eight months, but only now "anticipate[d] commencing interviews in the near future."

Apparently, that's how seriously the Department takes allegations of official misconduct: They respond by punishing the whistleblower.

Despite OPR's inexplicable delay in investigating my very serious allegations regarding destruction of evidence and obstruction of justice, their office somehow found time to refer me to the state bars in which I was licensed. The Justice Department had already blacklisted me in the legal community. They were now going after my very license to practice law. As Elaine Cassel of Civil Liberties Watch wrote about my situation:

> Ashcroft has struck back at people who went over his head to report misconduct of federal prosecution witnesses, one in a terrorist case, one not. Both professionals, both are facing sanctions from their professional bodies at this time. They absolutely did the right thing, in the name of principled justice. Ashcroft did not get the verdicts he wanted, in some measure because of the actions these professionals took. But he is getting back at them. Even if they are proven to have done no wrong (and experts I have spoken to believe that they are innocent of wrongdoing), the fact that they are under investigation must be reported to malpractice carriers and, in some states, to clients.

In addition to subjecting me to more investigations, the bar referrals (even absent a finding of misconduct) made law offices reluctant to hire me because it would automatically increase their liability insurance.

The OPR letter explained: "The Department believes that Ms. Radack violated her duty not to knowingly reveal attorney-client privileged information (i.e., confidential information of the United States) . . . by leaking internal Department emails regarding the Lindh interrogation to *Newsweek*." What about the Department violating its duty to preserve attorney-client privileged information and not selectively comply with federal court orders?

The referral letters themselves were based on the secret leak report, which was still under seal with the Lindh court and to which I did not have access. Let me repeat that: I was referred to the bars based on a secret report. I could identify with the Guantánamo detainees, who were far worse off, being held indefinitely on the basis of evidence they weren't allowed to see or challenge. It felt like something from the English Star Chamber.

The Department "summarized" the secret leak report and shared details of what the IG "determined" and what "the government concluded." The referral letters then added a curious footnote that "the information regarding the leak investigation contained in this letter is not 6(e) [secret grand jury] material," as if that somehow excused the Department's disclosure of information that was still under court seal. The government committed the same offense—disclosing materials under court seal to a non-government entity—of which it was accusing me. It was so hypocritical, on top of being vindictive. It also implied that the government had in fact taken the allegations against me before a grand jury; of course, there was no mention of the criminal case being dropped.

I was thirty-weeks pregnant. I couldn't eat or sleep and lost five pounds over about as many days—not a good thing when you're supposed to be gaining a pound a week. I had an emergency ultrasound to make sure the baby was still growing.

Rick Robinson wrote back to OPR that we found their letter both inadequate and disturbing. He pointed out the lengthy delay between when OPR first received my whistleblower allegations and OPR's latest stunt of referring me to the bars. Rick also pointed out how startling we found their admission that they had yet to conduct *any* interviews into my allegations; in fact, it was doubtful that they would have undertaken any further investigation but for the letter of inquiry Rick had sent.

It appeared, instead, that they had spent the last seven months investigating *me*—the very type of retaliatory activity we had hoped they would expose rather than perpetuate. The fact that they referred me to the bars without even having requested any information from me indicated that their office had little interest in knowing all the facts and circumstances surrounding my allegations of misconduct at PRAO.

More fundamentally, we had already disproved several of the key "facts" underlying OPR's bar referral, which is something of which their office should have been aware given that, by its own admission, it was working hand-in-glove with the IG. For example, I explained the facts surrounding the phone calls and fax transmission between Hawkins and *Newsweek* to my Hawkins supervisors, who interviewed me at the direction of the IG and then shared the information I provided with the IG. The bar referral was based on purely circumstantial evidence, including the same "smoking fax" the IG used earlier to get me effectively fired from Hawkins, which we already proved was nothing more than my law review article.

We copied the bars on a response we sent to OPR and explained that the Justice Department had no legal or factual basis for suggesting that I violated the confidentiality rule, and that its referral of me was just a continuation of a series of retaliatory actions in violation of the Whistleblower Protection Act and other federal laws.

A defensive OPR responded that they began their investigation of my allegations on March 7, 2003, and were prepared to commence interviews in May, but that they had to hold their investigation in abeyance because of the criminal investigation of *me*. This claim was a classic example of blaming the victim. If OPR had bothered to do even a cursory examination of my allegations in a timely and honest fashion, rather than waiting, the government would have concluded much earlier that it had no basis for criminally charging me and could have begun investigating those who were truly criminally culpable in this matter and who remain unexamined to this day. The government would have also unearthed evidence that was exculpatory to the bar referrals.

OPR disagreed that we invalidated several of the key facts upon which they relied, but did not give specifics and refused to withdraw the bar referrals.

Finally, OPR claimed that they did not violate the court's sealing order by providing the substance of the leak investigation to Bar Counsel, but as an apparent fallback position, insisted that they offered only "documentary evidence" that already "exists in Department files independent of the October 11, 2002 report"—a distinction without a difference. They even supplied inapt court citations in a vain attempt to justify their breach of a sealing order. Back-peddling from and downplaying their violation of the court's seal was just that—a thinly veiled attempt to cover up more misconduct.

*After* all this damage had been done, to add insult to injury, OPR announced that they were now, finally, ready to interview me as part of their investigation into my allegations.

Given that they would risk violating the court's sealing order so that they could provide false and defamatory information to the bar authorities, I couldn't realistically expect them to conduct an objective and thorough review of *my* allegations of misconduct at PRAO and of retaliatory actions by components of the Justice Department, which now, unfortunately, appeared to include their office. It showed extremely bad faith to shoot first and ask questions later. They referred me to the state bar authorities before investigating the conduct that formed the basis of those referrals. It is obvious that they had a vested interest in discrediting me in order to bolster their own accusations.

Six years later, OPR, now under the direction of Attorney General Eric Holder, Jr., issued a report clearing John Yoo and Jay Bybee—the authors of the "torture memos"—of professional misconduct allegations. The report initially concluded that Yoo and Bybee violated their professional obligations as lawyers when they wrote the main torture memo; however, career veteran David Margolis (one of Claudia's sponsors) softened that finding to say that they showed "poor judgment"—meaning OPR would not need to refer them to their respective state bar associations for potential disciplinary action. Holder later created a new unit to do what Margolis unilaterally did: Decide how to discipline officials who commit misconduct, including whether to refer them to state bar associations for punishment. It was just the latest example of redundancy in post-9/11 fixes.

The bottom line remained, though: The Justice Department referred me to the state bars, but not the authors of the torture memos.

And, the bar referral against me is still pending at the DC Bar more than eight years later—in 2012—despite a letter from the country's leading legal ethicists saying that it is unfounded.

# THE "NO-FLY" LIST

ON DECEMBER 24, 2003, military lawyers prepared a letter to the International Committee of the Red Cross, responding to its concern about conditions at the Abu Ghraib prison. The letter, signed by Brigadier General Janis Karpinsky, contended that isolating some inmates at the prison for interrogation because of their significant intelligence value was a "military necessity," and said prisoners held as security risks could legally be treated differently from prisoners of war or ordinary criminals. The result of this policy was that Abu Ghraib became a macrocosm of what happened to John Walker Lindh.

On December 28, I gave birth to a beautiful, perfect baby girl. The doctors administered a high dose of corticosteroids to me to try staving off an MS exacerbation, which I had experienced following the birth of each of my boys.

While I was still in the hospital, Bruce Fein filed the "Motion to Inspect" the government's secret leak report. The motion asked the judge in the Lindh case to unseal the report detailing the government's investigation of my conduct, which had been used to thoroughly smear me, and to appoint a special prosecutor to investigate the Department's contempt of court. In the motion, I revealed myself as *Newsweek*'s source and explained in detail why I was entitled to go to the press under the federal whistleblowing law. I also finally told my version of events—the condensed, impersonal, and sanitized "legalese" version of what I have written here. On New Year's Eve, we sent a copy of the motion to the state bar authorities as part of my response. It felt like a fitting way to begin 2004.

In March, my grandfather died in a fire, so I flew to Georgia for the funeral. On the way down, I was singled out for a full-body pat-down search and told that I had been "randomly selected." The screener asked me if I was wearing an underwire bra. I said yes. She said she would have to feel it for verification. I asked her to please not press too hard because I was breastfeeding and it would trigger my let-down reflex.

Meanwhile, my fashionable Medela "Pump in Style" was being sent back and forth through the x-ray machine.

"It's a breast pump," I explained. Attorney General Ashcroft, who ordered the Justice Department to cover the semi-nude statue of the Spirit of Justice, may have a problem with the female breast, but surely baggage screeners, many of them women, would be more enlightened.

When I later opened the luggage I had checked, the lock had been broken off and there was a note from the Transportation Security Administration (TSA) explaining that my suitcase had been hand searched. A plastic blue "lock" had been placed on the suitcase as a "courtesy." It seemed invasive, but tolerable because it was for security's sake.

During the return flight, I again had to undergo the extended dance version of the more extensive search.

Before my next flight less than a week later, I became aware that the airlines administered a "No-Fly" list—an early example of "security theater"—especially popular at the government monstrosity known as the Transportation Security Administration (TSA). These were measures intended to make people feel secure while doing nothing to actually improve security. The TSA puts on regular showings of its theater of the absurd, which involves audience participation of passengers in various stages of undress. My favorite incarnation: taking off your shoes while going through security because of a Christmas Day "shoe bomber" named Richard Reid, detected not by security, but by alert passengers.

Administered by airlines, the "No-Fly" list was designed, in theory, to keep terrorism suspects off commercial airlines. But in actuality, it subjected scores of innocent passengers to repeated interrogation, detention, and stigmatization. The "No-Fly" list is one of two maintained by the TSA, part of the Department of Homeland Security. The other is the "Selectee" list. Those on the "No-Fly" list are not allowed to board commercial aircraft. Those on the "Selectee" list must go through more extensive screening before boarding. Homeland Security officials will not confirm or deny that you are on the "No-Fly" list and will not discuss the criteria they use to put people on the watch list, except to say that it identifies people suspected of posing "a risk of air piracy or terrorism or a threat to airline or passenger safety."

When I went through security for my flight to California, I was again pulled aside for a full-body wand search. With respect to my carry-on items, they wanted to know why I had a breast pump but no milk and no baby. I politely explained that *that* was precisely the point: I couldn't bring my infant on the trip, so I planned to collect and store milk for her during my travels.

On the way back, the screeners looked at my boarding pass and I was again told that I'd been "randomly selected" for a more elaborate search. "Randomness" was becoming pretty predictable. Randomness, in the true sense of the word, has no specific pattern or objective. Randomness is a phenomenon that does not produce the same outcome or consequences every time it occurs under identical circumstances. Randomness is unsystematic.

I asked the screener if I was on the "No-Fly" list or the "Selectee" list. She said, "I can't tell you." It seems that if the answer were no, she would have just said so.

I had two full baby bottles of milk in the refrigeration compartment of my breast pump. A male screener asked me to take a sip from each. This was months before a similar scene appeared in Michael Moore's movie *Fahrenheit 9/11*.

"Are you serious?" I asked.

I asked to see a copy of the written policy in which passengers are asked to personally sample liquids they take through security. I figured that if there was a policy governing suspect liquids, the screeners would be uniformly applying it (as other passengers strolled by with their coffee cups) and that screeners would be equipped with sterile droppers from which they could take a sample of my breast milk to make sure it wasn't some kind of organic peroxide—an explosive with unusual stability problems. But these screeners were obviously not really concerned that my milk was, for example, perchloric acid—an odorless, watery-white liquid that can be dangerously reactive. If they harbored such a concern, they would not have asked me to open the bottles because they would have exploded.

Unsurprisingly, there is no basis for the drink-your-own-breast-milk test. At that time, passengers could take through security everything from beverages to hand lotion to nasal spray. Knowing there was no lactation policy, I again objected because drinking from the sterile baby bottles would contaminate the milk (which any nursing mother can tell you is like liquid gold.) Moreover, the milk was for the baby, I'm lactose intolerant, and it formed, overall, a barbaric request. At that point, the screener's supervisor said he would check the milk in a different way, which he did by rubbing a white cloth all over the bottles and the breast pump. I can only surmise that the cloth was meant to pick up traces of chemicals or hazardous material, which of course, it did not. I was finally allowed to board.

By now, I was certain that I was on the "Selectee" list, though I had no way of verifying that or of getting my name removed. This was the most over-the-top retaliation for blowing the whistle in a high-profile terrorism case. The "Selectee" list was just the latest example in which I had been designated as a suspect without any sort of due process. I shared the dubious distinction of being on the airplane watch list with the likes of Anthony Romero, then the executive director of the ACLU, Senator Kennedy, Cat Stevens, and various members of the Green Party. It was more than an inconvenience. It was political punishment.

Getting stopped twice in less than a week for secondary security screening measures seems *not* like a way to stop passengers who pose a real security risk, but more like a way to detain, interrogate, delay, embarrass, harass, and humiliate perceived political enemies. That's what happens when those in political power label dissenters as unpatriotic. Politics becomes a proxy for suspicion. Our nation's leaders fail to realize that it makes us all less safe to devote so much time and energy, and so limited resources, to vengeful partisan practices rather than going after people with *real* terrorist ties. The government's long campaign of investigation and harassment against me exemplifies the wasteful and anti-democratic nature of the Bush administration's ill-defined war on terrorism, which the Obama administration has taken up with equal fervor.

On April 28, 2004, Deputy Solicitor General Paul Clement argued three so-called "enemy combatant" cases before the Supreme Court. Justice Ruth Bader Ginsburg asked him a prophetic question: "Suppose the executive says, 'Mild torture, we think, will help get this information,'" she queried. "Some systems do that to get information."

"Well, our executive doesn't," Clement replied. "And I think the fact that executive discretion in a war situation can be abused is not a good and sufficient reason for judicial micromanagement in overseeing of the authority. You have to recognize that in situations where there is a way, where the government is on a war footing, that you have to trust the executive." Even though top military officials knew of the Abu Ghraib prisoner abuse at least as early as January 2004, defense officials deliberately hid knowledge of it from Clement, making him unwittingly mislead the Supreme Court.

With tragic irony, that evening, "60 Minutes II" aired the explosive photographs of detainees in the American-run Abu Ghraib prison outside of Baghdad, Iraq. The release of these photographs dovetailed with the May 10, 2004 issue of *The New Yorker*, in which Pulitzer Prize-winning journalist Seymour Hersh blew the Abu Ghraib prison abuse scandal wide open. These two events sent shock waves around the world. Hundreds of sadistic photos seeped out over the following weeks: Naked prisoners stacked in a pyramid, a female soldier leading around a nude captive by a dog leash, inmates with women's underwear over their heads, a hooded prisoner with electrodes attached to his fingers, and others too awful to describe.

A number of pivotal events like the Abu Ghraib scandal influenced my situation and validated the advice I originally rendered in the Lindh case. None of these events standing alone ended my ordeal, but taken together, they all worked to turn the tide of public opinion and prodded people to at least cast a jaundiced eye upon the conduct of the administration in the war on terrorism. The judicial branch stopped acting as a rubber stamp of whatever the executive branch did and, at long last, Congress showed some signs of life.

In addition to the explosive "60 Minutes II" segment and Seymour Hersh article, the torture memos started leaking out in a steady drumbeat of horror.

*Finally,* I thought with a sigh of relief. I cried tears of joy that I was no longer howling alone into the darkness with my complaint that the United States was taking shortcuts of the worst kind. But I also cried tears of despair that it was so much more widespread than what happened to John Walker Lindh. What happened to Lindh spread to the entire patchwork of oversees US detention facilities.

On June 1, 2004, James Comey, deputy attorney general for the Justice Department, held a news conference concerning US citizen Jose Padilla, a former Chicago gang member held by the US as an "enemy combatant" for two years. Comey had been the US attorney back when Padilla was first arrested on a material witness warrant—another law abused in terrorism investigations after 9/11. Instead of material witnesses being called to testify against others, frequently they were charged with crimes themselves—depriving them of constitutional protections (such as the reading of their Miranda rights) and holding them for lengthy and indefinite periods.

Comey's press conference was ostensibly in response to a letter from Senator Hatch requesting information about American citizens being held on US soil as enemy combatants. But the suspicious timing of the presser suggests that it was being used as a backdoor way to influence the Supreme Court, which was close to ruling on the case of Jose Padilla, an American "enemy combatant," and to deflect attention from a melodramatic presser given by the dynamic duo of Ashcroft and Mueller a week earlier—criticized by many for overstating the al Qaeda threat in order to influence the upcoming presidential election.

As I listened to the news conference, I couldn't believe my ears. Comey's words echoed exactly the concerns I originally voiced in the Lindh case.

"Why don't you bring criminal charges against him now?" a reporter asked.

"I'm not ruling out that criminal charges might be an option some day," Comey responded. "We, obviously, can't use any of the statements he's made in military custody . . ."

Really? Such a conclusion was not so obvious, or evident at all, to Ashcroft and Chertoff in the Lindh case.

When later asked if the government had plans to present the information from Comey's press conference to a grand jury, Comey reiterated the problem with that course of action:

> I don't believe that we could use this information in a criminal case, because we deprived him of access to his counsel and questioned him in the absence of counsel . . . This was done not to make . . . a criminal case against Jose Padilla. It was done to find out the truth about what he knew about al Qaeda and threats to the United States.

Comey got it. (He would later become the hero of an almost cinematic drama in which Bush administration officials tried to bully a hospital-ridden Ashcroft into authorizing sweeping domestic surveillance powers—that the Justice Department had already deemed unlawful—by doing an end-run around Comey, the acting attorney general. Comey raced to the hospital, where our country nearly had the greatest constitutional crisis since Watergate because he and other senior officials came within hours of resigning if their concerns were ignored.)

"How does your refusal to grant access to an attorney for [Padilla] throughout the process fit into this?" another reporter asked. "You have now indicated that he may have access, as I understand it, and . . ."

"And he's had access to counsel," Comey said.

"[T]hat being the case, if you're not going to bring charges any time soon, for reasons that you've explained, and yet he has access to counsel, where does that leave him in the long run?" the reporter followed up.

"I'm not [foreclosing] bringing a criminal case," Comey explained. "What I was saying was, I don't believe we can use his statements made in military custody against him. So if there's a criminal case to be made separate and apart from that, perhaps that's an option."

Comey seemed so principled. It spoke volumes that during the Bush years, being a hero, or being principled, simply meant obeying the law. Comey's statements about access to counsel and not mixing intelligence-gathering with criminal prosecution in a civilian court reflected exactly the concerns I expressed in the Lindh matter, and a complete reversal from what Ashcroft and Chertoff said and did two years earlier in the Lindh case.

A few weeks later, the government was caught off guard when the Supreme Court ruled in the trio of "enemy combatant" cases on June 28, 2004. While the Court affirmed the president's authority to detain enemy combatants in the war on terrorism, it ruled that the latter have the right to challenge their detention in US court and that they have the right to counsel. The ruling was a major blow for Bush.

In a six-to-three decision against the administration, the Supreme Court ruled that the more-than-600 detainees from over forty-two different countries held at Guantánamo Bay could appeal to federal courts, with the assistance of a lawyer, that they were being held unlawfully.

As for Padilla's case, the Court sidestepped the merits of his situation on a jurisdictional technicality.

But in the matter of US citizen Yaser Hamdi—who was captured alongside John Walker Lindh, on the same day, at the same place in Afghanistan—his case resulted in a landmark Supreme Court defeat for the White House. The Court ruled eight-to-one that Hamdi should have an opportunity to rebut before a neutral party the government's case for detaining him. Four Court members would have even released him, arguing that his detention was unlawful. Justice Sandra Day O'Connor wrote for the majority, "We have long since made clear that a state of war is not a blank check for the president when it comes to the rights of the nation's citizens." Significantly, she stated that Hamdi "unquestionably has the right to access to counsel," a question that had been at the heart of my advice in the Lindh case.

Less than four months after telling the Supreme Court that holding Yaser Hamdi in military custody was crucial to national security and the war on terrorism, the government released him scot-free back to Saudi Arabia, a hotbed of terrorism. John Walker Lindh is still serving his twenty-year sentence in a medium security prison facility in Indiana, which houses more than 200 inmates, all but two of whom are Arab Muslims. If proportionality is one of the penological purposes for punishment, then the Hamdi-Lindh disparity was an utter failure of justice.

On July 14, 2004, I reached a settlement with Hawkins, Delafield & Wood. The major sticking point had been their insistence that I forego my ability to write about my experience and their insistence on a "non-disparagement clause." I said that the truth was worth more to me than their money. The settlement preserved my right to speak, and I used the proceeds to pay off some of my attorney's fees.

As the Maryland Bar proceeded against me, in discovery we finally obtained a copy of the coveted IG report, which the Justice Department had used to tarnish my reputation with my law firm and with the bar associations. We had only procured a "summary" of it previously with Bruce Fein's motion.

The IG report provided more missing pieces of the puzzle. Just as Chertoff's judicial confirmation hearing began to answer the question of how high up the chain of command the malfeasance went in my case, and just as the torture memos filled in the backdrop of my story, the IG report answered the question of motive, about which I could only speculate before.

First, it contained an email that I had never seen in which De Pue told Patty Merkamp Stemler, Chief of the Criminal Division's Appellate Section, "[W]e have committed an ethical violation."

Second, and most importantly, it contained the sworn affidavit of John De Pue, someone I had often wondered about, but never dared to contact throughout this mess. In his sworn statement, he said, "[In] January 2002, Jim Reynolds," who was the Chief of the Terrorism and Violent Crime Section, "informed me that the Criminal Division's leadership was disturbed that I had sought PRAO's advice in this matter."

In a strange confluence of events, on January 11, 2005, with the Maryland Bar proceeding three days away, President Bush selected Michael Chertoff to head the Department of Homeland Security. That prompted another article by Eric Lichtblau for the *New York Times*. Not only did Eric use the article to document Chertoff's lies to Congress the last time around, but he was also able to get John De Pue to speak on the record about what happened. It was the first time De Pue had commented publicly:

> The front office was unhappy with the fact that I had gone to PRAO with my inquiry . . . I was more or less told that I was out of line in making that inquiry. It was not a popular thing to do, but I thought at the time it was the reasonable thing to do. We'd been told time after time that if an ethics issue arose, the people in that office were the ones to see.

De Pue made clear that "[t]he unhappiness was coming from Chertoff."

The next day, I had my hearing before the Attorney Grievance Commission of Maryland. The IG report played a significant and exculpatory role because it was so ludicrous, sloppy, and riddled with holes and contradictions. The Maryland Bar dismissed the case. Under reciprocal discipline ethics rules, the DC Bar should have done the exact same thing, but as this book goes to print in 2012—eight years later—the case against me in DC is still pending.

At Chertoff's confirmation hearing, Senator Akaka from Hawaii questioned him about the retaliation against me, and Chertoff pledged to protect whistleblowers, which made me groan. But the testimony that really infuriated me was when, upon being questioned about the infamous torture memo, Chertoff told Senator Carl Levin (a friend of whistleblowers and opponent of torture), "You are dealing in an area where there's potential criminal liability. You had better be very careful to make sure that whatever it is you decide to do falls well within what is required by the law."

Senator Levin continued his line of questioning and Chertoff continued to gild the proverbial lily:

> If you are dealing with something that makes you nervous, you'd better make sure that you are doing the right thing. And you'd better check it out, and that means doing an honest and diligent examination of what you're doing, and not really putting your head in the sand or turning a blind eye.

Chertoff's utter hypocrisy gave me the courage and fortitude to speak out. I did what I had been so scared to do for so long and wrote an op-ed for the *LA Times* about my experience and Chertoff's role. I said my piece, and there's something incredibly empowering about that. I was not going to sit in the corner and suck my thumb while Chertoff weaseled his way into yet another promotion. My op-ed was only eighteen paragraphs, but it was the most important thing I ever had written.

Chertoff was, of course, confirmed. During his tenure at the Department of Homeland Security from 2005 until 2009, I went through numerous incarnations of "redress procedures" to remove my name from the "No-Fly" list, but it was not until after his departure that I was able to board an airplane without automatic secondary security screening.

The day after Chertoff was confirmed, John De Pue, with whom I had exchanged the infamous emails, and *Newsweek* journalist Michael Isikoff, to whom I had disclosed them, met each other at a New America Foundation event on "The Torture Papers." Their presence there spoke for itself and the life-transforming nature of the John Walker Lindh case.

# EPILOGUE

PEOPLE ALWAYS ASK ME, "Knowing what you know now, would you still blow the whistle?"

My answer is yes. In a utilitarian sense, I realize this is completely irrational. It has wreaked havoc on my family, my health, my finances, and my career. But in a deontological sense, it is right. As Robert Frost expressed in his poem *The Road Not Taken*, "Two roads diverged in a wood, and I—I took the one less traveled by, And that has made all the difference."

In discussing whistleblowing, it disappoints and scares me when people I love, trust, and respect say, "I don't know if I could do it."

My response is, without meaning to sound self-righteous, "How could you not?"

Small whistles can make big noises. I was willing to take a career risk out of a deeper loyalty to the American people. I was committed to the government's mission to serve the public and do "justice." I was simply doing my job and got caught sideways in executive branch politics. My true employer was the American people, not a bunch of political ideologues.

We learn from our leaders how to dodge responsibility. It is frightening to think that so many people would stand by idly in the face of wrongdoing, rather than speak out. That is how we get days like 9/11 in the first place—by stifling meaningful dialogue and blinding ourselves to opposition. As we observe the ten-year anniversary of 9/11, which temporarily united our nation, we need to take a critical look at the perverse detour we've taken over the last decade. It has left our country weaker, more politically divided, and no longer an example to other nations.

After three and a half years of professional exile, Alan Grayson hired me to bring *qui tam* (False Claims Act) lawsuits, representing government contractors who were blowing the whistle on reconstruction fraud in Iraq. It provided a cathartic re-entry into the practice of law.

Two years later, Grayson ran for Congress and was elected US Representative for Florida's 8th district. I applied for a job as the director of National Security and Human Rights at the Government Accountability Project (GAP), the nation's leading whistleblower organization, which had helped me years earlier. It was a perfect fit.

That same year, Eric Lichtblau published his book, *Bush's Law*, which put the last missing piece of my puzzling ordeal into place:

> Providing documents to the defense could produce embarrassing details about Lindh's custody, and the White House knew it.
>
> Michael Chertoff, the Justice Department's criminal chief, got word through back channels that officials at the White House were meeting to talk about what to do about Lindh and the discovery issue. As would become more and more frequent, the Justice Department did not have a seat at the table; the discussion went on without them. A senior Justice Department official called Gonzales to find out

what was going on—and why the department charged with handling criminal prosecutions was not even involved. In a heated phone conversation, Gonzales made clear that the White House was calling the shots and that he, as White House counsel, had decided not to turn anything over to Lindh's defense lawyers in the way of documents. "We're not going to provide discovery," Gonzales said.

*So that's what happened*, I thought. How inconceivable it was, even today, to think that the White House ordered the Justice Department to withhold court-ordered discovery. I had obviously been caught cross-wise in a high-stakes turf fight between the Justice Department and the White House. And I had also stumbled upon one of the Bush administration's most controversial programs in its infancy: torture.

After Lindh, the administration learned its lesson and quickly changed course: Try terrorism suspects, both foreigners and Americans, in military commissions or not at all—a debate that still rages today. In December 2011, President Obama signed into law measures (contained in the annual military budget bill) that provide for indefinite military detention of alleged terrorists without charge or trial, including US citizens, anywhere in the world.

It was only while working at GAP that I came to fully realize how my ordeal in the Lindh case had prepared me for shepherding a similarly situated whistleblower, Thomas Drake, through an even darker ordeal on the blunt end of a federal criminal leak investigation and prosecution.

In April 2010, I read an article that immediately caught my attention. The short *New York Times* article stated:

In a rare legal action against a government employee accused of leaking secrets, a grand jury has indicted a

former senior National Security Agency official on charges
of providing classified information to a reporter . . . that
examined in detail the failings of several major N.S.A.
programs, costing billions of dollars, using computers to
collect and sort electronic intelligence. The efforts were
plagued with technical flaws and cost overruns.

Alarm bells went off in my head because just that short bit of text
told me that a government employee witnessed malfeasance, blew the
whistle on it, and became the target of a "leak investigation." (There
is no such actual crime of "leaking"; quite the opposite, we have a
free press in this country and citizens are free to speak.) It sounded
very much like my case; however, in this case, the government (now
under the Obama administration) went one step further and indicted
the former government employee.

The little I knew about the Drake case rankled me because Obama
came into office on a platform of openness and transparency. Federal
employees who had exposed wrongdoing or were considering doing
so had reason for hope after eight years of the Bush administration's
relentless retaliation. After being elected, Obama stated:

Often the best source of information about waste, fraud,
and abuse in government is an existing government
employee committed to public integrity and willing to
speak out. Such acts of courage and patriotism, which
can sometimes save lives and often save taxpayer dollars,
should be encouraged rather than stifled.

I campaigned for Obama, contributed to Obama, and voted for
Obama. And I believed him.

However, not only was the Obama administration's Justice Department now prosecuting a whistleblower, but it was also doing so under the heavy-handed and notoriously vague Espionage Act—a far-fetched idea advanced by a neoconservative. The Espionage Act is a World War I-era law meant to go after spies, not whistleblowers. Being charged under the Espionage Act automatically painted any defendant as a traitor—one of the most damning charges that can be leveled against an American.

I had immediate concerns for Drake because I knew first-hand that criminal leak investigations were often a pretext to harass people who had exposed government incompetence, ineptitude, and wrongdoing that proved, at best, embarrassing to the government and, at worst, criminal. I wrote an op-ed for the *L.A. Times* on the differences between whistle-blowing and leaking and how what Drake was alleged to have done fell in the former category. I put the op-ed out there as a beacon of sorts, hoping that he or one of his friends, relatives, or attorneys would see it.

A month later, Drake's mother called me and tried to enlist my support. I told her that anti-solicitation rules prohibited me from reaching out to her son directly, but that he was welcome to call me. As soon I spoke with Tom Drake, there was an instant connection born of our shared experiences. Career public servants who had the dubious distinction of becoming the targets of federal criminal "leak investigations" comprised an infinitesimally small number.

We met shortly afterward for coffee, across from the Apple Store, where he was now working as a wage-grade employee—a far cry from his six-figure salary as a member of the Senior Executive Service. Drake is a fifty-four-year-old man of thin build with dark blue eyes. He came across as serious, but he was also in disbelief about what the government was doing and how this could really be happening. He expressed both disappointment and hurt. I knew exactly how he felt. While I had met many whistleblowers over the years, never had I met someone whose circumstances so mirrored my own.

Almost immediately, despite the objections of his public defenders (he had been represented for years by a private attorney, but now qualified as indigent due to his enormous legal bills), I took him on as a client. As I learned more about the Drake case, I discovered that it was worse than I thought: He had dedicated the bulk of his adult career to military and government service, had a stellar record, and had done everything by the book in terms of blowing the whistle. Yet the government was clearly in overdrive, trying to put him in prison.

Around the time I was first giving advice in the John Walker Lindh case, the Saxby Chambliss-led subcommittee of the House Permanent Select Committee on Intelligence subpoenaed Drake as a material witness for its investigation into "Counterterrorism Intelligence Capabilities and Performance Prior to 9-11." This report was intended to be helpful to a broader Joint Inquiry that ensued, conducted by the House and Senate Intelligence Committees, into the intelligence community's activities before, during, and since 9/11; specifically, to ascertain why the intelligence community didn't know of the attacks in advance and to identify what might be done to better position them to warn of and prevent future terrorist attacks.

The Joint Inquiry subpoenaed Drake in the summer of 2002 as a material witness in its investigation, which eventually resulted in the "Final Report of the Joint Inquiry into the Terrorist Attacks of September 11, 2001." In September 2002, during the pendency of the Joint Inquiry, three retired NSA employees and a retired congressional staffer filed an IG Hotline complaint with the Defense Department about massive waste, mismanagement, and illegality at the NSA. Drake served as the unnamed "senior executive" because, while the complainants were all retired, he still worked at NSA and feared reprisal.

As a result of the complaint, an audit investigation followed that spanned the next two and a half years. In early 2003, the IG audit investigators formally contacted Drake as a material witness and person of knowledge regarding the substance of the complaint. He notified his supervisors and the NSA's own IG office, all of whom instructed him to cooperate.

As part of his cooperation, Drake participated in dozens of formal interviews and question-and-answer sessions, exchanged numerous phone calls and several hundred emails (including extensive electronic attachments of key documents relevant to the investigation) with the IG audit investigators, and delivered several thousand pages of hard-copy documents to them. He also provided large amounts of requested data and highly detailed information about massive and persistent fraud, waste, and abuse; violations of contractor regulations; violations of the Foreign Intelligence Surveillance Act; Fourth Amendment violations; and NSA's willful failure to provide accurate reporting to congressional intelligence oversight committees. The IG also asked him to review and comment on substantial amounts of material and to review notes and documents that came into the IG's possession from other sources and interviews during the course of the investigation, as well as rough drafts of the report they were writing.

The IG issued a several-hundred-page report on December 15, 2004, substantiating the concerns of Drake and the complainants; however, the IG immediately classified it, which made it unavailable to the public.

On December 16, 2005, Eric Lichtblau and his partner at the *New York Times*, James Risen, published their explosive story, "Bush Lets US Spy on Callers Without Courts," which exposed the NSA's ultra-secret domestic spying program. It thrust the country deep into a constitutional crisis with few parallels in American history. It is not hyperbole to say that both the intelligence community and the public were stunned by this revelation. President Bush, who would later dub the secret spying as the patriotic-sounding "Terrorist Surveillance Program," stated publicly, "My personal opinion is: It was a shameful act for someone to disclose this very important program in a time of war. The fact that we're discussing this program is helping the enemy."

Two weeks later, the Justice Department launched a large-scale investigation into the sources for the *Times* article. Privacy and civil liberties advocates quickly argued that the "leak investigation" should be replaced with an investigation of the warrantless wiretapping itself. The sprawling investigation included five full-time prosecutors and twenty-five FBI agents, cost millions of dollars, and is still ongoing. The government identified and targeted approximately 1000 people in the universe of possible sources, issued subpoenas for over fifty individuals, and raided fewer than a dozen of them—half of whom included Drake and the other four whistleblowers who had complained to the Defense Department IG.

The *New York Times* leak investigation is how Tom Drake landed on the government's radar screen. He initially drew the attention of investigators because the government believed he was a source for the *Times* article. Drake was *not* one of the *Times*'s sources and was never charged with being one of the *Times*'s sources. Yet he is the *first and only* person ever to be indicted as a result of the massive leak witch hunt.

In April 2006, one of the IG complainants, Diane Roark, notified Drake and the others that she was a target of the *New York Times* "leak investigation." Almost a year later, one of the other IG complainants, former NSA mathematician Bill Binney, met voluntarily and cooperated with the FBI's investigation on three occasions during the months of March through July of 2007. During all three meetings with the FBI, Binney took the opportunity to report a number of crimes committed by the NSA about which he had first-hand knowledge.

To their utter shock, on July 26, 2007, the FBI conducted simultaneous armed raids on the homes of all four of the Defense Department

IG whistleblowers. They all believed that the Department of Defense IG double-crossed them by providing the FBI with their identities and the fact that they had complained about certain NSA programs—information that by law is supposed to be protected so that Inspectors General can maintain their independence and whistleblowers will feel safe knowing that their complaints are confidential. The armed raids alone were indicative of the retaliation. FBI armed raids in white-collar investigations are done to intimidate, not for legitimate investigatory purposes.

Four months later, a dozen armed FBI agents fanned out across Drake's lawn and raided his home while his wife and twelve-year-old son were home. At the same time, another half-dozen agents raided his office at the National Defense University's Industrial College of the Armed Forces, where he was a visiting professor. The FBI hauled away personal possessions including family photographs, which had not been returned as of the summer of 2011. To add insult to injury, news stations showed up with large boom antenna vehicles late in the morning and the raid was broadcast on television that evening, later that night, and the next morning.

That same day, NSA tossed Drake into the black hole of administrative leave. The next day, NSA pulled his Top Secret/Sensitive Compartmented Information security clearance, which he had held for nearly twenty years—rendering him unemployable in the intelligence community. Unfortunately, I was all too familiar with the government casting you into the uncertain void of administrative leave and rendering you unable to work in your field of expertise.

Drake, like Binney, wanted to use the raid as an opportunity to report crimes committed by the government post-9/11, including NSA crimes that had gone unaddressed. He spoke with two FBI agents for eight hours on the day of the search, explaining his participation in the IG's investigation. He also explained how, more than a year after the IG investigation closed, he began corresponding with Siobhan Gorman, then a reporter with the *Baltimore Sun*, but never provided her with classified information.

Drake voluntarily met with the same agents two weeks later for about six hours at his home. They seemed fixated on and convinced that he had something to do with the damning *New York Times* story. They asked Drake about STELLAR WIND, the NSA cover name for a significant segment of the domestic surveillance program. Drake felt concerned immediately that the FBI wanted to discuss a highly classified program in unprotected space. "Where's the cone of silence?" he asked. The FBI did not care and insisted that he answer questions provided to them by the NSA.

Four months later, Drake again voluntarily met with the same two FBI agents, later to be joined by prosecutor Steven Tyrell, who explained how Drake would be charged for conspiring with the other IG whistleblowers to enter into "honest services fraud"—a popular catch-all with which to charge people on whom the government does not have anything incriminating—as well as charged under the Espionage Act and the Communications Intelligence Act. Tyrell attempted to have Drake plead guilty or spend "the rest of your natural life behind bars."

"I refuse to plea bargain with the truth," Drake stated.

Tyrell was not pleased. After that final cooperative meeting, though, the handwriting was on the wall. Drake lawyered up, retaining Tony Bisceglie—famous for having represented David Kaczynski, brother of the Unabomber, who wanted to turn in Ted Kaczynski but to avoid the possibility of the death penalty.

Drake's cooperation with the FBI on the three occasions before he retained counsel would prove to be his undoing. A couple of days after the final meeting, NSA presented Drake with a termination package that they wanted him to sign without reading. Instead, he voluntarily resigned, significantly, with no adverse action noted on his personnel record, an oddity if NSA thought he'd actually done something criminal.

On January 20, 2009, Barack Obama was sworn in as the 44th president of the United States. Elected on soaring rhetoric of transparency and reform, there was exuberant hope in the country that the dark Bush years were over. But in May 2009, more than a year after the first plea attempt, Tyrell again presented Drake with an outline for a plea agreement that the government might consider. Drake rejected the plea attempt for a second time.

Six months later, in November 2009, Drake's attorney requested an audience with Lanny Breuer (the head of the Justice Department's Criminal Division), Tyrell, and others to discuss Drake's case. At that meeting, Breuer introduced another prosecutor, William Welch II, who was going to take over the case and "give it a fresh pair of eyes."

Welch was no stranger to being in criminal jeopardy, having been arrested for driving under the influence of alcohol in 1997. He failed four field sobriety tests, but the charges were dismissed because a videotape of part of the traffic stop had been erased. Welch's criminal defense attorney said in court papers, "The destruction, loss, or sloppy, cavalier or negligent handling of the videotaping deprived him of potentially exculpatory evidence." But the lesson about the importance of a criminal defendant's right to exculpatory evidence appears to have been lost on Welch. In the botched prosecution of the late-Senator Ted Stevens of Alaska, the judge found Welch in contempt of court for not turning over exculpatory information, stating:

> That's outrageous for the Department of Justice, the largest law firm on this planet, to come before a federal judge and say, yeah, Judge, you know, we recognized your order . . . and we haven't gotten around to comply[ing]

with it, and we really don't have a good faith reason or any reason for not having complied with it.

The judge appointed a special prosecutor to conduct a contempt investigation, which recently resulted in a 500-page report validating that the prosecution's handling of the case was "permeated by the systemic concealment of significant exculpatory evidence."

For Welch, it was presumably a career-killer and possibly a crime. He was exiled back to Massachusetts, but it was not long before his patron, Lanny Breuer, resuscitated Welch's career and handed him the high-profile portfolio of leak cases left over from the Bush era. Perhaps it was a chance at career rehabilitation. If Welch did well, he restored his reputation, and if he failed, he could be written off as prosecutor with a tainted history. The more likely explanation is that Breuer knew that Welch was a pit bull willing to skirt the ethics rules. Whatever the reason, Welch was an odd choice because of his checkered past and because he had no prior experience with national security matters. In my days at the Department, it was unfathomable that such high-profile prosecutions would be handled by an attorney not seasoned in the relevant practice area.

In January 2010, Welch contacted Drake's attorney and informed him that the government was now pursuing a "different approach" to Drake's case. This led to Drake and his attorney meeting in March with Welch, one of the FBI agents, the lead NSA General Counsel lawyer for the case, and an NSA investigator. Welch briefed Drake on the revamped criminal case and included a plea outline as part of the presentation, which Drake again refused. The third time was not the charm.

The government indicted Drake on April 14, 2010, for alleged willful retention of classified information in violation of the Espionage Act, obstruction of justice, and making false statements. The Drake case thus entered the books as the fourth time in our nation's history that the government chose to force a trial for espionage on someone who is not a spy. (It speaks volumes that the first time was the infamous Pentagon Papers case against whistleblower patriarch Daniel Ellsberg.)

That was where things stood when Drake became my client. Even though Thomas Tamm and Russell Tice had confessed to being sources for the *Times* article in question, neither of them were prosecuted—much less indicted—and the government formally closed out its investigation of Tamm during the pre-trial phase of the Drake case.

After a number of long meetings with Drake, I began to realize just how extensive his whistleblowing was—he complained to his bosses, the NSA IG, the Defense Department IG, and the House and Senate Intelligence Committees. I had never seen someone blow so many whistles, or blow them so loudly. That was the first prong in my strategy of helping Drake: People needed to recognize him as a whistleblower. As a popular blogger on Daily Kos, I started to write about his case. A few blogs made the Recommended List, but most were overtaken by "trolls" and "Obamabots." Early on, I reached out to Ellen Nakashima of the *Washington Post*, who to her credit had already been following the case. I also reached out to Eric Lichtblau of the *New York Times*, and the reporter who was now covering Lichtblau's old beat, Scott Shane. In June, Shane published the first article ever about a phenomenon that has only worsened: "Obama Steps Up the Prosecution of Media Leaks." In July, Nakashima published a huge profile on Drake entitled "Act of Honor, or Betrayal?"—indelicately subtitled, "'Nuclear Option' Blew Up in Whistleblower's Face." Their articles clearly painted Drake as a "classic whistleblower." But it was a long haul to get the rest of the media on board.

Next, I wanted to introduce Drake to kindred spirits. I know how isolating the plight of a whistleblower is and I wanted him to know that he was not alone. He was adamant that I "be his voice" (since criminal defendants are told to keep quiet lest they accidentally incriminate themselves or make impeachable statements). I knew he needed all the allies I could muster. I introduced him to Dan Ellsberg, FBI whistleblower and *TIME Magazine* "Person of the Year" Coleen Rowley, FBI whistleblower Mike German of the ACLU, Jim Bamford (the world's expert on the NSA), Steve Aftergood (a critic of US government secrecy policy), and retired CIA officer-turned-political activist Ray McGovern. At the premiere of *Fair Game*, I introduced him to many others such as former Ambassador Joseph Wilson IV, Hamilton Fish, Conrad Martin, Randy Fertel, and Andy Breslau.

A number in the whistleblower community, good-government groups, transparency organizations, and civil liberties unions had their doubts about the Drake case because the government had done such a good job out of the box of tarnishing him with the loaded espionage label and propagating the meme that he "leaked classified information to a reporter." It was an uphill battle to get people to understand that he 1) never leaked classified information to a reporter and 2) was not charged with leaking classified information to a reporter. Oddly, he was charged with alleged retention—not disclosure—of classified information.

Even when reporters got the charges right, it was a Herculean effort to fight the government's narrative in the indictment that Drake willfully retained classified information "for the purpose of disclosure to a reporter." Even as this book goes to press, some reporters are still getting it wrong. This is exacerbated by the government's intentionally misleading statements, even after Drake's case eventually collapsed. For example, the Justice Department spokesman said, when discussing Drake, that there are available avenues for whistleblowers to report wrongdoing, even in classified matters, "and we encourage people to use them"—even though this is exactly what Drake did—"[b]ut people cannot make unilateral decisions to publicly release information that jeopardizes national security" . . . even though the government never alleged that Drake jeopardized national security.

Then I started to dig into the indictment. I knew that Drake was a test case for the Justice Department to try a novel legal theory—curiously, one espoused by a neoconservative named Gabriel Schoenfeld—that the Espionage Act could be used to prosecute leakers. Frustratingly, journalists did not seem worried about the slippery slope of the government's argument and the terrible precedent it could set for going after the media. Taken to its logical conclusion, the Espionage Act could not only be used to go after sources, but also reporters, newspapers, publishers, readers of any resulting article, and anyone to whom the reader passed on the article.

To my horror, of the five Espionage Act counts, the first two were red herrings because the evidence supporting both had been published, marked "UNCLASSIFIED," on the NSA intranet and both were available for viewing by thousands of people. The subject of count one dealt with a document entitled "What a Success." It was declassified in July 2010 (it was unprecedented for the government to declassify evidence before a case is completed because it undermines the very premise of the prosecution)—but the government continued to use it against Drake and did not tell the defense about its declassification for another eight months. The subject of count two was a document entitled "Regular Meetings," which had been posted on the NSA intranet and marked "UNCLASSIFIED"—exculpatory information that, again, Drake's defense team did not receive until ten months after the indictment was issued.

Even more egregiously, the other three espionage counts were based on information that in whole or in part Drake had provided to the Defense Department IG. The pieces of evidence supporting all five of the espionage counts were found in Drake's basement and were not deemed to be classified until *after* they were seized from his home and subjected to a "forced classification review." The Constitution prohibits the government from passing *ex post facto* laws, but apparently the Constitution is still out of vogue.

Obama had signed an order early in his presidency that all agencies were supposed to review documents to see what could be declassified after the rampant over-classification, retroactive classification, and new hybrid secrecy categories that proliferated during the Bush years. Instead, according to the Information Security Oversight Office, officials classified nearly 77 million documents in 2010, a forty percent increase over the year that Obama came into office. Instead of solving the problem, the government just increased it.

This is all the more dangerous while we have been fighting two wars because it's more important than ever to make sure that the information that needs to be protected is protected and that the system is not overburdened with information that shouldn't be in the classification system in the first place.

The country's classification czar under George W. Bush, J. William Leonard, came out of retirement to serve as an expert in Drake's case, and even once it crumbled, filed a formal complaint against the National Security Agency and Justice Department seeking punishment of officials who classified a document that he says contained no secrets. He explained on NPR: "In my thirty-four years, I've seen many egregious examples of what were classification but I have never seen a more deliberate misuse of the classification system as I did in this case." The Orwellian landscape had not changed. It just had a new leader.

As for the other counts, Drake was basically accused of four instances of "making false statements" for, in essence, telling the truth. The government just refused to believe him, despite his unwavering assertion that he never disclosed classified information to a reporter. And the single obstruction count was based on his refusal to cooperate further (his constitutional right) in what revealed itself to be a bad-faith, pretextual "leak investigation" that was not interested in solving who leaked to the *New York Times* (a dubious premise to begin with), but instead was clearly out to nail him.

My next order of business was to bullet-proof Drake and get some sunshine on this case. I had a multi-pronged strategic with list for that. Ideally, it would include Drake winning the Ridenhour Prize for Truth-Telling, an investigative article in *The New Yorker* by Jane Mayer, and perhaps a TV segment on "60 Minutes" or "FRONTLINE." I never expected that this trifecta would be realized.

My personal opinion is that, like in my case, the saving grace was the combination of excellent lawyering and the media—the vaunted Fourth Estate. The public defenders, Jim Wyda and Debbie Boardman, with the assistance of private attorney John Cline of the Wen Ho Lee case, did a stellar advocacy job. However, as in my case, once Jane Mayer devoted her behemoth and impeccable investigatory talents to digging into what was behind the scene, the government's house of cards started to collapse. Hundreds of articles followed in the mainstream media, the blogosphere, and academia—all of which just gained momentum the closer we got to trial in June. As Drake is fond of saying, it was not an "either/or" but a "both/and" situation—meaning it took *both* the lawyers *and* the media to win.

During a critical period in June, the judge issued a string of unfavorable rulings against the government and concurrently the media swung ninety-nine percent in favor of Drake. The *Washington Post* ran two editorials, a week apart, criticizing the case. Quite quickly, the government's hand went from bad to worse. On June 3, 2011, as the government contemplated appealing the rulings adverse to them or dismissing the charges completely after another bruising day, Welch approached one of the Maryland public defenders, Jim Wyda, in the well of the courtroom and opened discussions about Drake accepting a plea agreement. To the astonishment of the prosecution and his own criminal defense team, Drake rejected upward of six more formal and informal plea offers for almost a week until the government could actually find something to which he could legitimately plead guilty.

The public defenders were putting enormous pressure on Drake, and as his closest advisor, I racked my brain for something: Did he ever litter on NSA's campus or spit on the sidewalk? Did he ever park in the wrong parking space at Ft. Meade? He rejected a "Sandy Berger plea," similar to the one in which former White House national security advisor Samuel Berger pleaded guilty to a misdemeanor that acknowledged intentionally removing and destroying copies of classified documents from the National Archives. It simply didn't fit. Drake never sneaked documents out of NSA that were classified. The government eventually dropped all ten felony counts entailing up to thirty-five years in jail and he pleaded to a minor misdemeanor for "exceeding authorized use of a computer," an infraction for which the government promised to seek no jail time.

Drake was sentenced to community service and a year of probation. During Drake's sentencing, Judge Bennett had some choice words for the government, comparing its treatment of Drake to British tyranny in pre-Revolutionary War days:

> I find that unconscionable. Unconscionable. It is at the very root of what this country was founded on against general warrants of the British. It was one of the most fundamental things in the Bill of Rights that this country was not to be exposed to people knocking on the door with government authority and coming into their homes. And when it happens, it should be resolved pretty quickly, and it sure as heck shouldn't take two and a half years before someone's charged after that event.

In addition to the lengthy delay between the search and the indictment, the visibly perturbed judge noted, "and then over a year later, on the eve of trial, in June of 2011, the government says, whoops, we dropped the whole case . . . That's four years of hell that a citizen goes through. It was not proper. It doesn't pass the smell test." For those who might wonder, Bennett was appointed by George W. Bush.

Ultimately, Drake's case was built on sand and collapsed beneath the weight of the truth.

I wish I could say that the story ended there. But the Obama administration has three more Espionage Act cases teed up—against former State Department contractor Steven Kim, former CIA officer Jeffrey Sterling, and Army Specialist Bradley Manning. Despite the embarrassing setback in Drake's case, the Obama administration vowed to continue its war on whistleblowers—with a special emphasis on national security and intelligence whistleblowers (arguably the ones we need to hear from the most).

This public flogging of those who speak the truth to those in power does exactly what Welch said at Drake's sentencing that the government intended to do: Send a message. But this is a message of despotism, not democracy.

Drake and I both stumbled on and disrupted two of the most controversial policies of George W. Bush's in their early stages: torture and secret surveillance. The government attempted to justify both through a theory of expansive presidential power, enabled by a state-secrets doctrine that was used to evade judicial review.

We both complained through internal channels—our supervisors and respective Inspectors General—and, when that failed, made the difficult choice to go to the press anonymously. Then we became targets of federal criminal investigations into our disclosures. In effect, for exercising our First Amendment right to speak to the press about issues of public concern—revealing only unclassified information—we were designated as traitors and enemies of the state.

In reality, our "crimes" amounted to embarrassing the government by exposing high-level government malfeasance and illegality. Like the current crop of whistleblowers in the same boat, neither of us was alleged to have harmed national security.

When the Obama administration took office, each of us hoped that reason would prevail and that the persecution would stop. This wasn't reading too much into Obama's statements. He campaigned on abuses raised by whistleblowers and came into office hailing whistleblowers as courageous and patriotic.

Obama's actions have not matched his words. His administration's reaction to national security and intelligence whistleblowers has been even harsher than his predecessors. The Bush administration harassed whistleblowers unmercifully. But it took the Obama administration to actually prosecute them.

For a president whose mantra is to "look forward and not backward" when it came to investigating torture and warrantless wiretapping, it is brazen hypocrisy to resuscitate stale Bush-era cases for disclosures that served the public interest and did no harm to national security.

Using the Espionage Act to silence public servants who reveal government malfeasance is chilling at best and tyrannical at worst. This administration's attack on national security and intelligence whistleblowers expands Bush's secrecy regime and cripples the free press by silencing its most important sources. It's a recipe for the slow poisoning of a democracy.

Just after the signing of the Constitution, in answer to a woman's inquiry as to the type of government the Founding Fathers had created, Benjamin Franklin said, "A republic, if you can keep it." This is not the kind of republic I want to keep.

# ABOUT THE AUTHOR

Jesselyn Radack is currently the director of National Security & Human Rights at the Government Accountability Project, the nation's leading whistleblower organization. Previously, she served on the DC Bar Legal Ethics Committee and worked at the Justice Department for seven years, first as a trial attorney and later as a legal ethics advisor. Her writing has appeared in the *LA Times, Washington Post, Philadelphia Inquirer, Legal Times, National Law Journal, The Nation*, and numerous law journals. A graduate of Brown University and Yale Law School, she lives in Washington, DC with her husband and three children.

CPSIA information can be obtained at www.ICGtesting.com
Printed in the USA
LVOW041133060512

280541LV00003B/69/P